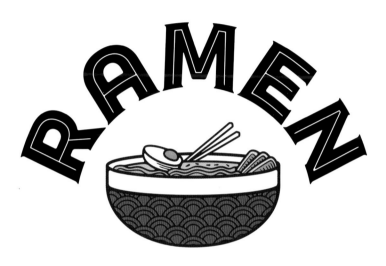

RAMEN

This book is dedicated to my cousin Masahiko, who used to take me to the best ramen shops in Tokyo when we were young. It is these memories that have helped me to create so many ramen recipes. Sometimes we would drive outside of Tokyo whenever he found a place for better ramen! I hope he likes my recipes as much as the ones we discovered on our adventures!

Published in 2023 by OH! Life
An imprint of Welbeck Non-Fiction Limited, part of Welbeck Publishing Group.
Offices in London, 20 Mortimer Street, London W1T 3JW, and
Sydney, 205 Commonwealth Street, Surry Hills 2010.
www.welbeckpublishing.com

Text © Makiko Sano 2023
Design © Welbeck Non-Fiction Limited 2023
Photographs by Simon Smith © Welbeck Non-Fiction Limited 2023
Cover image: Shutterstock Alexandra Leikina/James Pople.

A CIP catalogue record for this book is available from the British Library.

ISBN 978-1-83861-167-5

Publisher: Lisa Dyer
Copy editors: Emma Bannister and Theresa Bebbington
Food stylist: Pippa Leon
Props stylist: Morag Farquhar
Design: James Pople
Production: Marion Storz

Printed and bound in China

10 9 8 7 6 5 4 3 2 1

RAMEN

80 EASY NOODLE BOWLS AND BROTHS

MAKIKO SANO

OH!
LIFE

CONTENTS

THE RAMEN REVOLUTION 6

BUILDING A BOWL 10

THE NOODLES 12

CLASSIC DISHES 16

TOPPINGS & CONDIMENTS 18

TARES, BROTHS & TOPPINGS 24

CHICKEN & DUCK RAMEN 40

PORK & BEEF RAMEN 64

SEAFOOD & FISH RAMEN 104

VEGAN & VEGETARIAN RAMEN 126

INSTANT RAMEN *PLUS* 146

INGREDIENTS & SUPPLIERS 166

INDEX 170

ABOUT THE AUTHOR 174

CREDITS 175

THE RAMEN REVOLUTION

Ramen, the slurpable, Japanese staple, has become a
phenomenon in the West, a viral hit on TikTok and
YouTube and a food festival favourite.

Though we may think these moreish noodles come
from the shores of Japan, the roots of ramen are in
the country's larger neighbour, China. *Shina soba*,
one of the earliest forms of the dish, translates as
'Chinese buckwheat noodles', and noodles have
been a crucial Chinese staple since the earliest Han
period – around 202 BCE! They even have cultural
relevance. Chinese longevity noodles, eaten at the
lunar new year, require that you slurp the noodles
without biting them to guarantee good luck for the
following year.

According to the Shin-Yokohama Ramen Museum,
ramen was introduced to Japan at the end of the
Edo period (around the 1870s) when Chinese
immigrants arrived at the port towns of Yokohama,
Kobe, Nagasaki and Hakodate, and Chinese cuisine,
including noodle dishes, spread fast. Ramen became
popular owing to its easy, affordable and filling
noodle-laden broth – although the bowls would
have looked very different from today's versions –
simpler and without the array of toppings. Sold by
restaurants, food carts and street vendors, ramen
was aimed at students, night workers and after-hours
drinkers in search of a tasty snack.

But it wasn't until after the Second World War, when Japan was struggling with basic food supplies, that the large quantities of wheat flour sent over as aid from the USA resulted in a boom in noodle production. Noodles became known, along with other staples of Japanese cooking such as gyoza, as 'stamina food'. After the war, people would queue to buy black-market noodles, the noodles made from the newly received wheat flour rather than traditional rice flour. By the late 1950s, what had been seen as an affordable café food or street food was making its way into Japanese home kitchens as a time-saving and tasty meal option.

So how did we arrive at instant noodles – that pot of Asian flavours available whenever and wherever

Opposite above: A noodle bar in Tokyo.
Above: David Chang's Momofuku Noodle Bar in New York City.

we like? It's down to a Taiwanese businessman, Momofoku Ando, who was working at Nissin, a food manufacturer in Japan. Seeing the potential for an instant version of noodles and broth, he developed a way of drying and packaging noodles and the all-important soup flavouring mix, so that they could be rehydrated with boiling water in moments. In 1958, the instant noodle under the brand name Chikin Ramen was born. Not only was Japan booming by now but so was its love of all things technological and innovative. The packet noodle caught on and, by 1963, 200 million servings of the instant meals were being sold annually.

Ramen bowls, with their four core elements – sauce, soup, noodles and topping ingredients, had the potential for experimentation and creativity. Unlike the more revered, traditional Japanese technique of sushi-making, young chefs embraced ramen because they could play with its umami broths and customizable toppings. The diversity of noodles throughout Asia added even more fuel and inspiration to the trend, such as Korean guksu noodles (*Janchi guksu*), often flavoured with kimchi, Filipino pancit noodles (stir-fried noodles with a savoury sauce), Vietnamese noodles and the spicier Indonesian types. Regional and quirky twists on the basic elements can be found all over social media too, with Korean hot-dog ramen and Japanese Kewpie mayo noodles just some of the latest must-makes.

By the mid-2000s, ramen restaurants had begun to spring up in the trendsetting food hubs of Los Angeles and New York City. It wasn't long before the rest of the world was clamouring for its own noodle bars. Today, packets of noodles, Japanese condiments and broth stock powders can be found in many Western supermarkets, and self-service ramen bars are appearing in South Korea, where customers can mix or match their noodle selection, add individualized toppings or get a ready-made dish straight from a vending machine. The Ramen Revolution is here!

Left: A ramen noodle restaurant in the Shinjuku district of Tokyo.

BUILDING A BOWL

I create my recipes using authentic Asian ingredients. Many of these are widely available in Asian supermarkets and specialist shops, especially those in urban areas. Of course, you can swap out some of these ingredients for more readily available ones as you like.

~~~~~~

Although some simpler and speedier ramen dishes require very few ingredients, there are always four cornerstones to a bowl of ramen. These elements are layered together to give you that array of taste and texture that signals great ramen. Once you have mastered this basic construction form, you can build your ramen dishes with confidence.

TARE

A highly concentrated sauce or seasoning paste, *tare* means 'dipping sauce', and it is usually placed in the bowl before pouring over the broth, so that it swirls and mingles with the broth to enhance its flavours. Tare delivers the salty, savoury hit that takes ramen from tasty and nourishing to deeply flavoursome. This paste can be broken into three types: *shoyu*, or soy sauce, which was added to the original Chinese noodle recipes that came to Japan to disguise their meaty scents (as up until then Japanese people rarely consumed meat); *shio*, meaning 'salt', which often contains lemon and is used in much the same way as we do in the West, to amplify flavour and taste; and

Above: Toppings add colour, texture and crunch to your bowl.

miso, a deeply umami-flavoured sauce made from mashed soybeans, salt and *koji*, a fermented cooked rice.

BROTH, OR DASHI

Dashi, meaning 'extracted liquid', is the clear broth or stock in which most ramen noodles float. A dashi is always made from intensely umami ingredients to give a distinctive hit of flavour that stands out in contrast to the plainness of the noodles. An amber, golden or milky soup base, dashi roughly divides into three groups: broths made with animal-based ingredients, such as chicken, pork or beef bones; broths made with seafood-based ingredients, such as bonito flakes (a fermented and dried skipjack tuna that is also known as *katsuobushi*) and dried sardines; and broths made with vegetarian, earthy ingredients, such as shiitake mushrooms and kombu, a type of sea kelp.

NOODLES

Ramen noodles form the substance and bulk of every bowl. They can be divided into six types according to their thickness: ultra-thin, thin, medium-thin, medium-thick, thick and extra-thick noodles.

Ultra-thin and thin noodles are characterized by their smoothness. They mix well with the soup, making them the perfect choice for most ramen bowl recipes. It's also why the packets of shop-bought instant noodles, which tend to be skinny, work so well.

TOPPINGS

One of the delights of a ramen bowl is the endless accompaniments that can be used to top it. Consisting of protein and vegetables that sit on the tare, broth and noodles, toppings can be hot or cold additions: marinated meats, boiled eggs, leafy pak choi (bok choy), melted gooey cheeses, crunchy radish or dried seaweed, pickled ginger, sesame seeds, a dash of chilli oil or strictly vegan options; the list goes on. What you choose is really down to your own personal taste and dietary preferences.

CHOOSING THE RIGHT BOWL

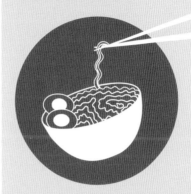

Bowl size and shape will make the most of how good your finished ramen looks once the toppings are added to the surface. A good bowl will also enhance the 'eatability' of your finished dish. The bowl needs to be big enough to hold all the elements of the ramen without spillage.

Look for reasonably deep bowls with gently angled sides – which help when fishing out noodles with chopsticks – and bowls with a wide enough opening to display toppings across.

The most common sizes used by restaurants are 20.5–23 cm (8–9 in) wide. However, bowls that are a little smaller will work perfectly well for a standard packet of instant ramen and a few accompaniments.

THE
NOODLES

In this book, I have given you noodle suggestions for each recipe; however, there are no hard and fast rules when choosing a noodle type for your ramen dish. Different regions have their own favourite options, but, just as with Italian pasta dishes, noodles are more often chosen depending on the sauce you are making. Lighter shio- and shoyu-flavoured dishes are suitable for any type of noodle you prefer. Skinny, ultra-thin straight noodles are the go-to for hearty tonkotsu-style broths, as they cling together, holding the richer broth well. Wavy noodles are perfect for miso-based ramen dishes, as they collect the miso seasoning flavourings beautifully.

My preference is for fresh or frozen fresh noodles. Frozen noodles are great to keep in a freezer drawer and use as and when you need. Fresh noodles and frozen fresh noodles are usually found in Asian supermarkets and sometimes in larger Western stores. If you can't find fresh noodles, then instant or dried packets of somen or soba noodles, or instant ramen noodle packs, will do just as well. Just make sure you stick to the cooking times indicated on your chosen noodles packet.

RAMEN (CHUKAMEN)

In Japan, the most common ramen noodles are called *chukamen* and they can be long and cylindrical, curly, squared or flattened. They are made by kneading wheat flour, salt, water and *kansui* – a mineral-rich, alkali water – together. Kansui gives noodles their bouncy elasticity and their yellowish colour. In China, eggs are sometimes used in place of kansui.

Kaedama!
(Extra noodles please!)
Remember this word if you want
an extra helping of delicious noodles
to add to your ramen bowl.

Traditional ramen are not gluten-free, but you can easily find gluten-free varieties where the wheat flour is replaced by rice, potato or millet flour.

SOMEN

Also called *somyeon* or *sùmiàn*, these are super-thin noodles made from wheat-flour dough. The dough is mixed with vegetable oil and stretched into thin strands before being air dried. They are highly versatile and frequently used in ramen bowl dishes. Their slimness also allows them to cook speedily.

SOBA

A popular, thin Japanese noodle found in fast food places and restaurant dishes, soba is made from buckwheat and looks a little more 'rustic' in colouring than other noodle types. These noodles work equally well in hot soups or chilled with dipping sauces.

Noodles get their shape by hand-cutting or snipping the dough, by hand-pulling and stretching the dough into long elastic strands, or by using cutting machines.

HIYAMUGI

A very thin wheat noodle, these are slightly thicker than somen noodles and can be used in the same way, especially for chilled and dipping ramen or summer dishes. Predominantly a white noodle, you may see some with pink, brown or green hues.

UDON

Considered the ultimate in comfort food in Japan, udon are made from wheat flour. These bouncy, chubby noodles are much thicker than other ramen noodles, but they can be used in soup broths where they are known as *kake udon*. They don't contain egg, so they make a great (and filling) vegan option.

There are also some interesting regional varieties of udon, many of which have become popular on social media. The *kishimen* noodle is a flat, wide noodle from Nagoya in Aichi Prefecture, while the *himokawa* udon is a super-wide, super-thin flat noodle, from the Kiryu area in Gunma Prefecture.

CHINESE GLASS NOODLES

Originating in China and found all over Vietnam, where they are known as *mien*, Chinese glass noodles are also known as transparent, cellophane and bean thread noodles. Depending on their origin, they are made from different base ingredients; for example, glass rice noodles are made from rice flour and water, while cellophane noodles are made from mung bean flour and water. The noodles are usually served with a savoury soup base and you can buy tubs of glass noodle soup base powders from Asian supermarkets to use as part of your broth seasoning.

FRESH NOODLES

In most high-end ramen restaurants, fresh noodles are almost always the preferred choice. Richer and tastier than their instant alternatives, and more yellow in colour, these freshly made, non-dried noodles hold their texture and bounce best. If you want to buy fresh ramen, then check the frozen aisle in your supermarket or local Asian food market. I use frozen fresh ramen in many of the recipes in this book.

DRIED NOODLES

The large packets of dried noodles sold in your local Asian store and supermarket tend to be dried noodles. These are made by drying freshly made, uncooked noodles. They are an excellent choice for any homemade noodle dish. Look for thin, straight styles (that look like spaghetti) where possible, as they produce the best results. There are also specialist soba noodles: green tea, or *cha*, soba (far left, above) has a light, naturally green colour, while the pink ume soba has Japanese plum added to the dough.

INSTANT NOODLES

The all-too-familiar single-serving packets of instant noodles are actually dehydrated from par-cooked noodles, which is why they take the shortest length of time to rehydrate and prepare. To choose an instant version that is closest to traditional ramen, cost will give you a good indication of quality. Cheaper versions are deep-fried prior to dehydration, while costlier versions are par-cooked and then air dried. An added bonus of instant noodle packets is the accompanying seasoning sachet that gives you a super-fast broth. I sometimes use these seasoning sachets along with other ingredients to build the flavours in my recipes.

CLASSIC DISHES

In this book, you will find lots of inspirational recipes to help you create your own tasty ramen bowls, but here are five classic dish styles that other variations are usually built around.

TONKOTSU RAMEN

Fukuoka in Japan is considered the home of unctuous and delicious tonkotsu. Slow-cooked pork bones are always the foundation of this ramen dish's base and give it a characteristic creamy, cloudy look.

MISO RAMEN

The Sapporo region in the northernmost part of Japan is the birthplace of deep-golden miso ramen. It takes its name from its star ingredient, miso, which gives the broth deeply savoury, umami flavours. Good grocery stores will usually stock the three main types: white, or *shiro*, miso is the mildest version and slightly sweet; red, or *aka*, miso has the longest fermentation time, which gives the most pungent flavour; and yellow, or *shinshu*, miso is a happy medium and consequently considered the most versatile. I have used white miso in the recipes.

SHOYU RAMEN

Shoyu, or soy sauce, ramen is one of the earliest styles of ramen and still one of the most popular versions. The soy element isn't just added to the bowl as a condiment; it is cooked and infused into the broth base and reduced to a brown tinted stock. With its salty, herbal aromas, it makes a great foundation for chicken and vegetable ramen dishes. For the most part, I use dark soy sauce, which is more flavoursome than the light version, in my recipes, but in several I use both, as you shall see.

SHIO RAMEN

Shio, or salt, ramen is a light and transparent style. It is often made with chicken bone broth and enhanced with seafood ingredients, such as dried sardines, dashi stock and bonito flakes.

TSUKEMEN

Tsukemen is a dish of 'dipped noodles', cooked then plunged into cool water, served alongside a bowl of tare ramen sauce. The noodles are served in a separate bowl and twirled and dipped into the sauce dish, sucking up the flavours and letting the thick soup coat each strand in tasty moisture. Because the dishes are served separately, the noodles tend to be cooler than the steaming broth-filled bowl. They can also be served as a chilled dish.

Opposite above: Shio ramen, with its light broth base.
Opposite below: A creamy tonkotsu broth ramen bowl.

TOPPINGS & CONDIMENTS

The toppings are the show-offs in your ramen bowl, elevating its look and visual appeal, which is an essential element in all Japanese cookery. They are the key to adding extra texture and dialling the flavour up another notch. Here is my guide to the finishing touches.

CHASHU

Roasted or braised, thinly sliced pork belly, chashu (also seen as *cha shu*) is the star among ramen ingredients and makes an appearance in many recipes, both hot and cold. You will often find it marinated or cooked with extra flavour enhancers to bring out the juiciness and delicious taste. *(See recipes on pages 32–33.)*

BOILED EGGS

Once halved, white and golden eggs add a beautiful touch to a ramen bowl as well as additional protein. Just passed soft-boiled is the ideal, with the yolk still a little runny. This nearly cooked yolk adds creaminess and richness to the noodle broth.

Ajitsuke tamago means 'seasoned egg', and it is a soft-boiled egg that has been marinated for several hours in a soy sauce and mirin solution. The result is a lightly salty and sweet egg with a golden, liquid yolk. *(See recipe on page 37.)*

VEGETABLES

Not only is there a wide variety of ramen-friendly vegetable options but they are also affordable and can make a ramen bowl vegan-friendly. Vegetables with good texture, such as bean sprouts, spinach, cabbage, onions and chives, go well with richer, creamier ramen broths. Usually they are lightly boiled or quickly stir-fried to retain their fresh, crunchy texture.

KAMABOKO

A Japanese steamed cake made from puréed white fish, which is then pounded into a paste and formed into the roll or cake, *kamaboko* can be sliced and used to top a bowl of ramen in much the same way as chashu. It has a distinctive pinkish red line around the outer edge, adding to its visual appeal. The version known as *narutomaki* is swirled pink. You will need to buy it from Japanese supermarkets, but it stores in the fridge for up to nine days once opened.

MUSHROOMS

Fungi are an essential ingredient in ramen cookery for their umami flavour, resistant texture, soft colour and attractive shapes. That flavour also makes them the ideal meat substitute. I use many varieties, including shiitake and *kikurage* (wood ear mushroom), or you might like to try the pale slender enoki. Dried mushrooms require soaking for 20 minutes or more to rehydrate before use. Cut off and remove the stalks (stems) to trim, but save them to use in broth stocks.

SWEETCORN

A popular topping with children, the pleasant texture and sweet flavour go well with the richness of the ramen. Along with eggs, sweetcorn adds a pop of colour and, of course, it's an ingredient you can keep in your freezer or kitchen cupboard, so it is always at hand as a last-minute option.

SEAWEED

The edible seaweed used for ramen cookery is dried. You might hear of several popular types: kombu, a type of sea kelp, comes in largish flat strips; nori, which are larger sheets often used to wrap sushi rolls; and wakame, which are thinner strips often used in miso-based soups and dishes. While kombu is often used in broth- or stock-making, wakame is more often used as a topping. All seaweeds add an ocean-like, savoury and salty note to a dish.

SPRING ONION (SCALLION)

The zingy, refreshing flavour and crisp texture of spring onions work beautifully with ramen! They complement other flavourings such as soy sauce, miso, tonkotsu (pork-based ramen) and shio (salty ramen) beautifully. Throughout this book, you will find recipes with the greens of spring onions used in the broth and nearly always a smattering of chopped spring onion scattered over a finished ramen bowl.

MENMA

Fermented or pickled bamboo shoots that have first been dried in the sun, *menma* is usually sold in jars at Asian supermarkets, but you can also find them vacuum-packed. Like spring onions, they are an essential ingredient in ramen. Slightly crunchy, their pickle flavour adds a bright burst of freshness and zing to enhance a bowl of broth and noodles. Think of them as the Japanese version of gherkins. You can also eat them as a snack or starter (appetizer).

KIMCHI

An increasingly popular ramen topping, particularly for home-made instant ramen, kimchi are slices of Chinese cabbage fermented in a mix of sugar, salt, garlic, chilli and optional *nam pla* (fish sauce). The resulting crunchy cabbage and vinegary juice are a perfect addition to ramen – simply fork some of the cabbage over the top and add a little of the fermenting juice.

RADISH

Daikon, meaning 'big root', is the general name given to radish in Japan, and it is also known by the Chinese name of mooli. Although from the same family as the small, red varieties you see in the West, the Asian version is large, white, milder, sweeter and

less piquant. Thinly sliced, it makes a crunchy ramen bowl topping. For colour, choose the purple version or the green skin and bright pink flesh of the Chinese watermelon radish (*see below left*).

UMEBOSHI

Umeboshi are pickled Japanese ume fruit (*Prunus mume*), considered a Japanese plum. Extremely sour and salty, they go very well with the earthy, meaty flavours of pork. Simply drop one or two whole umeboshi into your finished ramen bowl.

GINGER

Fresh ginger root is gloriously warming and spicy, and it can be grated raw or bought as a purée and squeezed from the tube.

Japanese pickled ginger is edible straight from the jar, even though technically it is still uncooked. The rose pink or golden slivers of ginger are a crunchy, refreshing garnish that adds sweet, sour and warm spice notes to your noodle bowl.

CHILLIES

Chilli flakes are a common ingredient to add to ramen, as are fresh red and green chillies. They add flecks of colour over the top of a bowl of noodles.

SRIRACHA

A popular chilli-based condiment made from chilli paste mixed with vinegar, garlic, sugar and salt, sriracha can be dotted over ramen. But be mindful and add spice to your bowl bit by bit, so you can adjust spice levels to what you enjoy.

INGREDIENT KNOW-HOW

Here are a few specialist ingredients to add extra flavouring to your ramen dishes.

DIAL UP SALTY INTENSITY

Mentsuyu, sometimes called *tsuyu*, is an intensely flavoured, liquid Chinese soup stock made from bonito flakes, kombu and soy sauce. It is used in much the same way as a stock (bouillon) cube to add depth of flavour and it can be diluted to different strengths to make the broth.

ADD CITRUS SHARPNESS

Yuzu kosho is a fermented spice paste made with salted chilli peppers (most often bird's-eye chillies) and the rind of the yuzu fruit (a sharp-tasting Japanese citrus fruit). It is used to add zesty flavour to light broths. It can be added to your ramen as a condiment or stirred into the broth for a pop of citrus.

CRANK UP THE SPICE

Gochujang is a Korean red chilli fermented paste that is spicy and sweet. Add a touch in the base of your bowl or stir into your broth for a kick of heat. *Gochugaru* is a Korean red chilli powder to scatter over your ramen; it has smoky, slightly sweet, fruity notes with a hot kick.

SCATTER ON MORE FLAVOUR

Furikake is a blend of dried nori, toasted sesame seeds, sugar and salt, but it varies from region to region. There are different flavourings available, such as wasabi and shiso. Traditionally, it is used in rice bowls and hot noodle dishes. *Shichimi togarashi* is a hot and spicy blend of red chilli pepper, orange peel, black and white sesame seeds, hemp seeds, poppy seeds, ground ginger and seaweed.

SOY SAUCE

In Japanese ramen, soy sauce is used to create the dashi broths. You might be familiar with light soy sauce, which is used when you want a light-coloured broth, or dark soy sauce, which is used for a more intensely salty flavour. These are Chinese versions of soy sauce. Japanese soy sauce is somewhere in the middle and a blend of soy and wheat. The soy sauce used in most of the recipes is the Japanese type, the most famous brand being Kikkoman.

SESAME SEEDS

Bursting with vitamins and minerals, sesame seeds (both white and black) are an everyday addition to lots of Japanese dishes. You can also buy toasted white sesame seeds, or toast them yourself at home. Sesame seeds can be added whole, scattered directly over the top of your ramen bowl to finish it, or finely ground in a pestle and mortar to incorporate into a soup base. They go especially well with the nutty, earthy flavour of miso ramen.

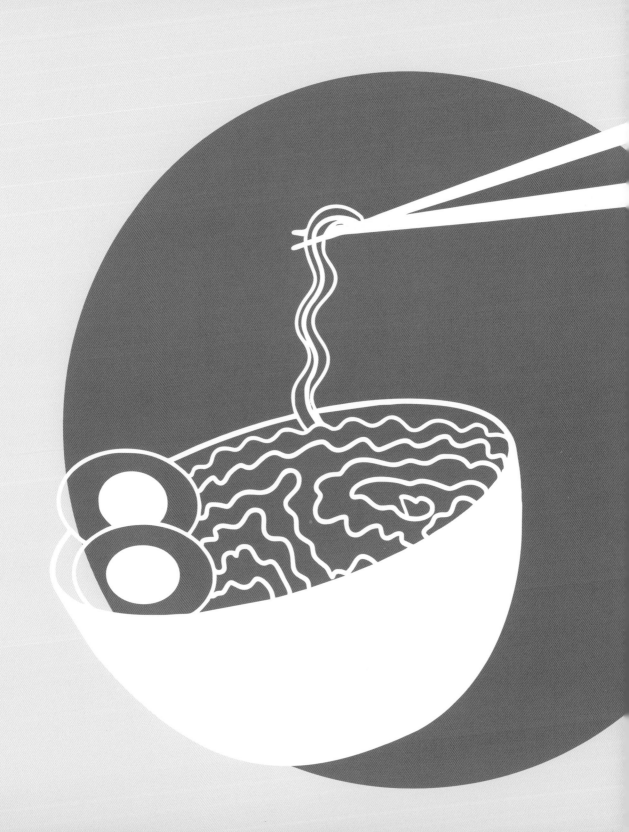

1
TARES, BROTHS & TOPPINGS

The building blocks of all ramen, tares (the seasoning sauce placed at the bottom of the bowl before ladling in the broth), broths and toppings can form endless combinations. Here you will discover a range of tare and broth recipes from clear light shoyu broths to deep rich tonkotsu, as well as the flavourful toppings and condiments you can add to customize the bowl recipes in the following chapters.

CHICKEN DASHI

Serves 4

A tasty, simple stock consisting of just two ingredients, this dashi is cooked long and slow for intense flavour. It is a typical Japanese stock and creates a very clean base for your ramen bowls.

~~~~~~~~~~~~~~~~~~~~~~~~~~~~~~

900 g (2 lb) chicken carcase or bones
1.8 litres (60 fl oz/7½ cups) water

Place the chicken in a pot, cover with the water and bring to the boil. Reduce to a simmer and cook for 3 hours, skimming off any scum as needed throughout the cooking time. The broth doesn't have to be perfectly clear as it all adds to the umami flavour.

Alternatively for a faster result, use a pressure cooker and reduce the cooking time to 1 hour.

Strain through a sieve into a storage jar or container. Seal and store in the refrigerator for up to 5 days.

> All the dashi recipes can be cooked in larger batches and frozen for use another time. Use within two months.

PORK DASHI

Serves 4

Pork dashi lies at the heart of the Japanese tonkotsu ramen. It is essential to use the correct pork bones, so the collagen and marrow can be released and deliver the creamy colour and rich, deep flavour.

~~~~~~~~~~~~~~~~~~~~~~~~~~~~~~

1 kg (2¼ lb) pork knuckles, pork hock or pork shin (shank)
1.5 litres (50 fl oz/6⅓ cups) water
3 whole bunches (about 24) spring onions (scallions), roughly chopped
5 cm (2 in) fresh ginger root, sliced
3–4 cloves garlic
1 large white onion, roughly chopped with peel on
240 ml (8 fl oz/1 cup) cooking saké

Rinse as much residue from the pork as you can, transfer to a pot and cover with water. Bring to the boil, then reduce to a simmer and precook for 30–40 minutes, skimming off any scum. Discard the water and rinse the knuckles thoroughly again.

Fill a pot with the water, add the pork, spring onions, ginger, garlic, onion (with peel) and saké. Simmer at a rolling boil for 7–8 hours, topping up the water when it gets low. Stir occasionally.

Strain through a sieve into a storage jar or container. Seal and store in the refrigerator for up to 5 days.

Opposite, left to right: Fish Dashi, Vegan Dashi and Pork Dashi broths.

VEGAN DASHI

Serves 5

This dashi base gets its umami taste from the rich flavour of shiitake mushrooms. It is simple to make, but it does need to be made the day before to give it time to rest.

〜〜〜〜〜〜〜〜〜〜〜〜〜〜〜

4 litres (140 fl oz/4¼ quarts) cold water
80 g (3 oz) dried kelp leaf (kombu)
5 dried shiitake mushrooms
3 medium white onions, cut into wedges
1 whole red chilli pepper

Add the cold water, kelp leaf and shiitake to a large container and leave to soak overnight, covered with a lid or cling film (plastic wrap), in the refrigerator.

The next day, transfer to a pot, add the onions and red chilli and simmer on a low heat for 30 minutes.

Strain through a sieve into a storage jar or container. Seal and refrigerate for up to 5 days.

〜〜〜〜〜〜〜〜〜〜〜〜〜〜〜

In ramen fish broths, dried kelp (kombu) and bonito fish flakes (*katsuobushi*) are used for flavour. Dried fish, such as sardines, known as *niboshi*, are also included for intensity.

FISH DASHI

Serves 4

Fish stock is one of the primary broths in Japanese cooking and combines the traditional ingredients of kelp and bonito flakes to create a deep umami flavour.

〜〜〜〜〜〜〜〜〜〜〜〜〜〜〜

20 g (¾ oz) dried sardines (*niboshi*)
8 g (¼ oz) dried kelp leaf (kombu)
20 g (¾ oz) bonito flakes (*katsuobushi*)
2.2 litres (77 fl oz/9½ cups) water

Clean the dried sardines by removing the heads and any black residue from the belly first, as they can make your stock taste bitter. Moisten a piece of kitchen paper towel and lightly wipe the kelp leaf surface.

Place the dried sardines, kelp and water in a large deep pot to soak for about 1 hour, then transfer to a medium heat and cook for 1 hour, reducing the heat a little once it simmers. Reduce the heat to low and cook for a further 20 minutes. Skim off any white foam on the surface stock from time to time as it cooks.

Remove the sardines and kelp from the broth with a slotted spoon. Add the bonito flakes to the broth and heat gently for 5 minutes, removing any surface foam as it cooks. Finally use a straining sieve to scoop out the bonito flakes, being careful not to squeeze them to avoid bitterness.

Decant into a storage jar or container. Seal and store in the refrigerator for up to 5 days.

TARE SAUCE

Serves 10–12

For an authentic addition to ramen, add a concentrated tare sauce to your bowl first; this will mix with the dashi when you pour it in, adding unique flavours and complexity.

~~~~~~

800 ml (28 fl oz/3⅓ cups) dark soy sauce
100 ml (3½ fl oz/scant ½ cup) light soy sauce
2 tablespoons apple cider vinegar
380 ml (13 fl oz/1⅔ cups) mirin
45 g (1½ oz/3 tablespoons packed) brown sugar

Mix all of the ingredients together in a saucepan and warm over a medium heat for 30 minutes. Allow to cool, then transfer to a storage container and refrigerate for 1 week to allow the flavours to develop. Use within 4 weeks.

To use in ramen, add 1–2 tablespoons to each bowl before adding the dashi, then the noodles and toppings.

~~~~~~

Tare is a thickened, reduced sauce made of intense seasoning ingredients that enhances the lighter dashi broth. It can also be used to season other soups, stews, stir-fries and dressings, especially those with meat or fish ingredients.

SHIO TARE

Serves 10–12

Shio tare is a salt seasoning to add to a ramen bowl. The umami flavours are amped up with the addition of dried shrimp and mushrooms; the tare needs to be made the night before.

~~~~~~

60 g (2 oz) dried kelp leaf (kombu)
30 g (1 oz) dried shrimp
30 g (1 oz) dried scallops (conpoy)
40 g (1½ oz) dried shiitake mushrooms
1.5 litres (50 fl oz/6⅓ cups)
200 ml (7 fl oz/scant 1 cup) mirin
300 ml (10 fl oz/1¼ cups) cooking saké
40 g (1½ oz/3 tablespoons packed) brown sugar
250 g (9 oz/1 cup) sea salt

Place the kelp, shrimp, scallops and shiitake in cold water to soak overnight. Drain and add to a saucepan with the water. Cook over a low heat for 20 minutes. Scoop out the kelp and strain through a sieve.

Pour the strained liquid back into the pan and heat gently, adding the mirin, saké, brown sugar and sea salt, stirring to dissolve. Cook the broth over a medium heat for 90 minutes, then allow it to cool.

Transfer to a storage container and keep in the refrigerator overnight before using. Use within 4 weeks.

To use in ramen, add 1–2 tablespoons to each bowl before adding the dashi, then the noodles and toppings.

AROMATIC OIL

Makes 975 ml (34 fl oz/4 cups)

A garlic-chilli condiment, this aromatic oil is typically added to your finished ramen dish before eating. It is essential for the ramen experience, as adding a little fat in the form of an oil imparts complexity, flavour and 'mouthfeel' to the dish, and it helps the broth cling to the noodle.

~~~~~~~~~~~~~~~~~~~~~~~~~~~~~~~~~~

15 g (½ oz/2 tablespoons) sliced garlic
20 g (¾ oz/⅓ cup) chopped spring onion (scallion)
20 g (¾ oz/3 tablespoons) chopped white onion
975 ml (34 fl oz/4 cups) rice bran oil
1 whole dried red chilli

Add the garlic, spring onion and white onion to a wok or pan. Add the oil and heat to about 160°C (320° F), using a kitchen thermometer, then slightly lower the temperature.

When the ingredients have turned golden, add the dry red chilli. Cook until the edges of the chilli are blackened, remove from the heat and strain. Decant the fragrant oil into an airtight jar or bottle, seal and store in a cupboard for up to 3-4 months.

To use, drizzle over ramen dishes as desired.

CHILLI OIL

Makes 450 ml (16 fl oz/2 cups)

Chilli oil, or *la-yu*, is a sesame-based oil infused with chilli flakes, often used in Chinese-influenced dishes such as ramen, stir-fries and gyoza (a type of dumpling). This chilli oil recipe is a 'must-make' for when you want to add a kick of heat to your ramen – just drizzle it over a finished noodle bowl.

~~~~~~~~~~~~~~~~~~~~~~~~~~~~~~~~~~

20 g (¾ oz/scant ¼ cup) *gochugaru*
(Korean red chilli powder)
40 g (1½ oz/scant ½ cup) chilli powder
10 cloves garlic, sliced
4 teaspoons sesame oil
360 ml (12½ fl oz/1½ cups) rice bran oil
10 whole black peppercorns
1 whole dried red chilli

Put the *gochugaru* and chilli powder in a bowl and dissolve with a little water. Meanwhile heat the garlic, sesame oil and rice bran oil over a medium heat before adding the peppercorns and dried red chilli. When the chilli starts to blacken, remove the pan from the heat. Allow to cool for a moment, then add the *gochugaru*-chilli powder mixture.

Once cooled, carefully pour the oil into an airtight jar, seal and store in a cupboard for up to 3-4 months.

Opposite, left to right: Chilli Oil and Aromatic Oil.

PORK CHASHU

Serves 2

In Japan, chashu or *nibuta*, as it's sometimes known,
refers to the simmering, braising cooking process used
to prepare the dish. This tasty pork recipe undergoes a
long marinade before roasting to make a tasty, satisfying
and hearty addition to a bowl of ramen.

100 g (3½ oz/½ cup) granulated sugar
70 ml (2½ fl oz/⅓ cup) dark soy sauce
1 tablespoon cooking saké
2 tablespoons oyster sauce
1 teaspoon grated garlic
1 teaspoon grated fresh ginger root
1 teaspoon white miso paste
500 g (1 lb 2 oz) pork shoulder loin

In a small bowl, mix the sugar, soy sauce, saké, oyster sauce, garlic, ginger and miso paste together. Add to a saucepan and gently cook over a low heat for about 7 minutes until the sauce has reduced and thickened slightly. Place the pork loin in a ziptop bag or sealed container.

When the liquid has cooled, pour it into the bag with the pork loin, seal and marinate in the refrigerator overnight or, ideally, for 1–2 days. Turn halfway through the marinating process to ensure all the meat is coated.

An hour or two before roasting, remove the bag from the fridge to allow the meat to come to room temperature. Preheat the oven to 200°C (400°F/Gas mark 6). Take the pork out of the marinade and place it on a wire rack over a baking sheet or grill (broiler) pan in the oven for 40 minutes, turning it halfway through the cooking time.

Meanwhile add the remaining liquid from the bag to a saucepan and simmer until reduced by half. Strain to make the sauce.

Once the pork is done, remove from the oven and allow to rest, then slice into 5 cm (2 in) thick slices. (If you like, refrigerate the meat first for an hour to make slicing easier.) Use the slices to top your ramen bowls. The sauce can be poured over the pork slices or used as a dipping sauce.

CHICKEN CHASHU

Serves 2

These chashu (sometimes written as *cha shu*) are chicken
rolls and a twist on the popular pork belly roll. Braised
in a soy sauce mix, the meat is tender and succulent.
Try this quick and easy accompaniment on top of your
favourite noodles to make a hearty ramen dish.

4 boneless chicken thighs with the skin
   on, about 120 g (4¼ oz) each
30 g (1 oz) fresh ginger root
2 spring onions (scallions), green
   ends only
3 tablespoons mirin
3 tablespoons Japanese soy sauce
2 tablespoons cooking saké
1 litre (35 fl oz/4¼ cups) water

Trim any excess fat or sinew from the chicken thighs. Thinly slice the
ginger with the peel on and cut the green part of the spring onions into
10 cm (4 in) lengths.

Make a cut down the middle of each chicken thigh and spread them out
flat, skin-side down, so they are an even thickness. Starting at one end,
roll up and tie tightly with kitchen twine.

Fry the thighs in a frying pan over a medium heat until the outer
skin is browned. Then add in two-thirds of the mirin, soy sauce, saké
and ginger. Pour in the water and warm over a medium heat. When
it reaches a boil, cover with a lid and simmer over a low heat for 40
minutes until cooked through. Add the spring onions to the pan and
boil for about 5 minutes more to reduce. Then add in the remaining
mirin, soy sauce and ginger and simmer over a medium heat until the
juice is reduced by half and thickens.

Allow to rest, then slice into easy-to-eat sizes and arrange on a plate.

Overleaf: Rolled pork chashu (left) offers a succulent,
melt-in-the-mouth addition to ramen, but for an easy
option, use pork loin slices (right) to top your bowl.

MISO MINCE

Serves 6–7

Miso is produced by fermenting soybeans into a thick paste. It is used to make sauces and spreads for pickling, as well as for mixing with dashi soup stock for soup or ramen. Nothing gives food an umami flavour like this savoury Japanese condiment, and this miso-pork topping shows off the unique taste.

～～～～～～～～～～～～～～～～～～

100 ml (3½ fl oz/scant ½ cup) sweet soy sauce
100 ml (3½ fl oz/scant ½ cup) dark soy sauce
4 tablespoons white miso paste
50 ml (2 fl oz/scant ¼ cup) cooking saké
1½ teaspoons rapeseed (canola) oil
500 g (1 lb 2 oz) minced (ground) pork
½ teaspoon ground black pepper

Mix the sweet soy sauce, dark soy sauce, miso paste and saké together in a small bowl.

Pour the rapeseed oil into a frying pan and warm it over a medium heat before adding the minced pork. When the meat becomes pale grey in colour, pour in the sauce mixture. Bring to a simmer and add the black pepper. Once all the liquid in the pan has reduced down, the dish is complete.

Serve 2–3 tablespoons on top of each bowl of ramen.

VEGAN MINCE

Serves 6–7

Rather than simply using processed soy protein as a pork substitute, this recipe reflects a more Japanese approach to meat-free eating by using natural produce directly. The result bursts with flavour; the umami deepness of mushroom is enhanced with miso, the tang of soy and balanced with savoury sweetness.

～～～～～～～～～～～～～～～～～～

450 g (1 lb) shiitake mushrooms
450 g (1 lb) shimeji mushrooms
6 tablespoons white miso paste
3 tablespoons cooking saké
3 tablespoons granulated sugar
1 tablespoon soy sauce
1½ tablespoons sesame oil

Prepare the mushrooms by trimming the stalks (stems) and finely chopping both stalks and caps.

Place the miso, saké, sugar and soy sauce in a bowl and mix well.

Heat the sesame oil in a frying pan over a medium heat and add the mushrooms. Fry for 3–4 minutes, stirring, until tender. Add the seasoning mixture and stir-fry until the flavours have absorbed and the mushrooms are sizzling lightly. Remove from the heat and top on your ramen.

SOY-MARINATED EGG

Makes 10

A classic topping for ramen bowls, soy-marinated boiled eggs are a delicacy that adds an unctuous richness and saltiness to your dish. The eggs are nearly always cooked to just past a soft boil to retain some of the gooeyness of the yolk when sliced in half to serve.

~~~~~~

10 medium (US large) eggs
750 ml (26 fl oz/3 cups) water
120 ml (4 fl oz/½ cup) dark soy sauce
45 ml (1½ fl oz/3 tablespoons) mirin
40 ml (scant 1½ fl oz/3 tablespoons) cooking saké
1 teaspoon chicken stock powder (or ½ stock/bouillon cube)

Bring water to a boil in a saucepan, gently add the eggs and cook for 6½ minutes. Immediately transfer them to a bowl of iced water (this will make it easier to peel off the shell) for 5–7 minutes, then peel.

Add the water, soy sauce, mirin and saké to a saucepan and bring to the boil. Once boiled, turn off the heat, add the stock powder, mix well and allow to cool.

Place your shelled eggs in a high-sided dish and pour the sauce over to cover. Let marinate in the refrigerator for 12 hours and then enjoy.

SPICE-SEASONED EGG

Makes 4

In Japan, versions of marinated or seasoned eggs used to top ramen are called *ajitsuke tamago* or *ajitama*. *Aji* translates as 'taste', and *tama* as 'ball' (or 'egg'); in other words, a ball of taste! This is a simple recipe that can be prepared in advance, and the eggs will keep in the fridge for up to three days.

~~~~~~

4 medium (US large) eggs
50 g (2 oz/1 cup) roughly chopped spring onions (scallions)
2 sachets instant ramen seasoning soup base
Sea salt and ground black pepper
1½ teapoons sesame oil

Bring water to a boil in a saucepan, gently add the eggs and boil for 7 minutes. This will create a medium-firm boiled egg. Immediately transfer to a bowl of iced water for 5–7 minutes, then peel.

Place the spring onions, dry ramen soup base, salt and pepper, and sesame oil in a ziptop sandwich or freezer bag. Secure and shake to mix. Add the soft-boiled egg to the seasoning and spring onion mixture, seal the bag and refrigerate for at least 3 hours.

To use as a topping for your ramen, slice the eggs in half and add to each serving.

BASIC RAMEN RECIPE

Serves 1

Once you have a supply of dashi broth bases, tares, noodles
and aromatic oil ready to go in your fridge, ramen will become
a weekly staple. Perfect for a last-minute, light supper or quick
lunch, this basic ramen recipe can be adapted to use any of the
tares, broths and toppings in this chapter.

150 g (5¼ oz/1 nest) frozen fresh ramen
    per person, or any noodles
    of your choice
300 ml (10 fl oz/ 1 ¼ cups) Chicken, Pork,
    Fish or Vegan Dashi (*see pages 26–28*)
15 g (½ oz/1 tablespoon) Tare Sauce or
    Shio Tare (*see page 29*)

TOPPINGS
Toppings of your choice
    (*see pages 18–23*)
Aromatic Oil (*see page 30*)

Prepare and cook your favourite noodles, following the instructions on
the packet. At the same time, warm up a portion of your dashi soup base
in a microwave or saucepan.

Put a tablespoonful of tare in the bottom of a serving bowl. Pour over the
broth so the two mingle. Add a portion of noodles to your bowl and then
finish with any toppings you like and a drizzle of oil.

It is usually the transparency of the dashi broth that
dictates what type of ramen to pair it with. Delicate
fish and vegetable dishes favour clear fish, chicken
or vegan dashi. Shoyu (soy) and shio (salty) ramen
typically are made with chicken dashi, even when
you are using other meats to top. Pork dashi is used
in heartier ramen bowls, like the creamy tonkotsu.

CLASSIC SHOYU RAMEN

Serves 2

Shoyu, or soy sauce, ramen is a versatile mainstay recipe and, fittingly, soy sauce is the star of the show, providing a deeply comforting and complex base layer of flavour. If you have pre-stocked your fridge and freezer with chicken dashi and pork fillet tenderloin, then you can whip up this dish with ease.

800 ml (28 fl oz/3⅓ cups) water
2 tablespoons Japanese soy sauce
1 tablespoon Chicken Dashi (*see page 26*)
1 teaspoon oyster sauce
1 teaspoon grated garlic
Sea salt and ground black pepper
100 g (3½ oz/1 cup) bean sprouts
240 g (8½ oz/2 nests) fresh Chinese noodles

TOPPINGS
4 slices roasted pork (shop-bought or Pork Chashu, *see page 32*)
2–3 spring onions (scallions), sliced
6 shoots *menma* (fermented bamboo shoots)
1 medium (US large) soft-boiled egg, halved

Begin by making the soup base. Put the water, soy sauce, chicken dashi, oyster sauce, garlic and a pinch each of salt and pepper in a saucepan. Cook over a medium heat until it comes to the boil, then add in the bean sprouts and simmer briefly.

Meanwhile boil the noodles in a separate pot, according to the instructions on the packet. Once cooked, drain thoroughly in a colander.

Place the noodles in 2 serving bowls, pour over the broth and top with the roasted pork, spring onions, bamboo shoots and boiled egg.

Shoyu ramen was invented in 1910 at a noodle shop called Rairaiken in Tokyo, the first ramen restaurant in Japan, which served 3,000 customers a day at the height of its popularity. The dish was a simple nourishing broth with noodles and quality ingredients that were adjusted according to availability.

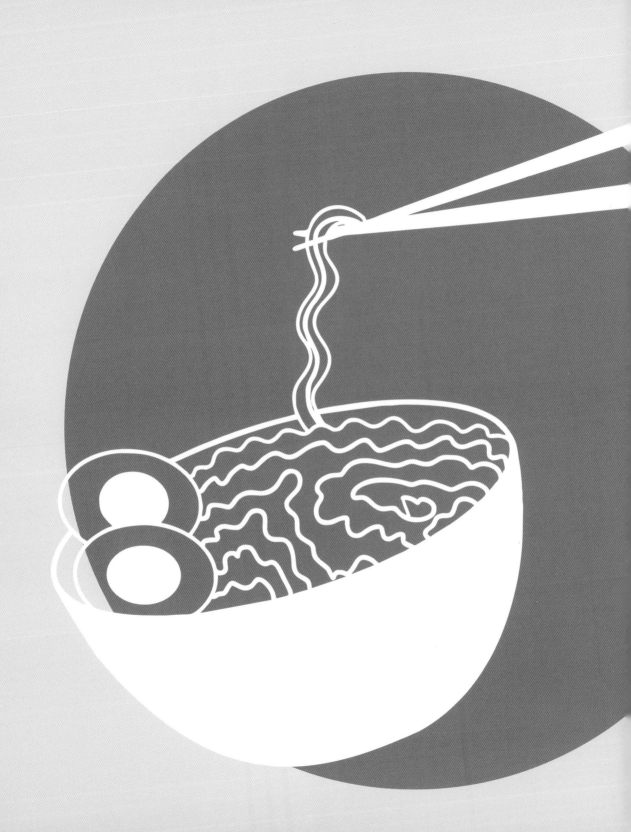

2
CHICKEN & DUCK RAMEN

In Japan, chicken is a popular ingredient in dishes, and locally grown chickens (*jidori*) are often pedigree breeds, prized for their flavour. Duck (*kamo*) forms the heart of many autumnal casserole-style dishes with mushrooms and clams. Both chicken and duck are incredible ingredients to top a ramen bowl, with myriad ways to prepare and enjoy them. Discover just how versatile poultry is with the recipes on the following pages.

CHILLI MISO RAMEN

Serves 2

The trend for chilli ramen originated in South Korea, where spice is used both for preservation and taste. As the spicy noodles reached the shores of Japan, fusion recipes started to emerge. The addition of miso here adds a distinctly Japanese twist to this dish.

300 g (10½ oz) frozen fresh ramen noodles
1 tablespoon sesame oil
240 g (8½ oz) minced (ground) chicken
1 tablespoon ginger purée
1 tablespoon garlic purée
400 ml (14 fl oz/1⅔ cups) water
1½ teaspoons white miso powder
1½ teaspoons *gochujang* (Korean red chilli paste)
1 teaspoon Japanese soy sauce
2 teaspoons granulated sugar
1 tablespoon cooking saké
1 teaspoon chicken stock powder
2 spring onions (scallions), chopped
2 tablespoons ground sesame seeds

TOPPINGS
Chinese chives, chopped
Fresh red chilli, sliced
Wakame seaweed, rehydrated for 5 minutes in cold water

Boil the ramen noodles as instructed on the packet, then plunge into iced water to firm them up. Set aside.

Heat the sesame oil in a frying pan over a medium heat. Once hot, stir-fry the minced chicken, ginger and garlic until the chicken is cooked through. Add the water to the pan and bring to the boil, then reduce the heat. Now add the miso powder, *gochujang*, soy sauce, sugar, saké, chicken stock powder and spring onions. Cook over a low heat for 2–3 minutes, stirring gently.

To serve, place your noodles in a bowl and top with the chicken and soup mix. Add the ground sesame seeds and mix gently. Top with the chives, chilli and wakame.

Miso paste is often the go-to ingredient in Japanese households, as it is closest to the natural soybean form. However, miso powder has a near-identical flavour profile and lasts longer, making it a better storecupboard option.

COLLAGEN RAMEN

Serves 2

Japan was one of the first countries to promote health and beauty from within. The collagen contained within fattier cuts like these chicken wings gives the recipe its health benefits.

~~~~~~

1 clove garlic
5 cm (2 in) fresh ginger root
1 kg (2¼ lb) chicken wings
4 spring onions (scallions), sliced
100 ml (3½ fl oz/scant ½ cup)
   cooking saké
3 litres (100 fl oz/12½ cups) water
Sea salt and freshly ground pepper
240 g (8½ oz/2 nests) fresh Chinese
   noodles

TOPPINGS

2 slices roast pork (shop-bought or Pork
   Chashu, *see page 32*)
1 medium (US large) boiled egg
Spring onions (scallions), green part
   only, sliced
Other toppings of your choice
   (*see pages 18–23*)

Crush the garlic with the flat side of a knife. Peel and thinly slice the ginger root.

Put the chicken wings, spring onions, crushed garlic, sliced ginger, saké and water in a large pot and heat over a medium heat, bringing it to a gentle boil. Reduce the heat and simmer for 1–2 hours, stirring, until the soup becomes cloudy. Strain the broth and discard the solid ingredients. Put 600 ml (20 fl oz/2½ cups) of the broth back in the pot to warm through. Season with salt and pepper to taste. Save the remaining stock for another recipe.

Boil the noodles in water according to the instructions on the packet. Drain and divide between 2 serving bowls.

Pour the chicken broth over the noodles. Arrange the roast pork slices on top. Halve the boiled egg and place a half on each bowl. Scatter over the sliced spring onions and add any other of your favourite toppings.

RAMEN SALAD

Serves 2

While we often think of ramen as a steaming bowl of noodle-laden broth, chilled salad ramen dishes make a refreshing summery meal. Cold ramen is a speciality of Hokkaido, home of Mount Yoteii, a lookalike of the famed Mount Fuji.

8 mixed green lettuce leaves
1 tomato
1 Spice-seasoned Egg (*see page 37*)
2 x 170 g (6 oz) chicken breast fillets
1 tablespoon cooking saké
240 g (8½ oz/2 nests) fresh Chinese noodles
45 g (1½ oz/2 cups) rocket (arugula)

SESAME DRESSING
2 tablespoons mayonnaise
2 tablespoons sesame oil
2 tablespoons ground sesame seeds
2 tablespoons Japanese soy sauce
2 teaspoons sugar
2 teaspoons rice vinegar

TOPPINGS
Daikon (mooli), julienned
Chilli flakes

Trim the ends of the lettuce leaves, then slice the leaves into bite-sized pieces. Cut the tomato into 6 wedges. Cut the egg in half.

Remove and discard any sinew from the chicken breasts and place in a heat-resistant container. Sprinkle with the saké, cover loosely with cling film (plastic wrap) and heat in a 800W microwave oven for 1 minute 10 seconds. Leave to cool, then slice the chicken.

Bring a saucepan of water to the boil and add the noodles. Cook according to the instructions on the packet. Drain and rinse under cold running water.

Make the dressing. Put the mayonnaise, sesame oil, ground sesame seeds, soy sauce, sugar and vinegar in a small bowl and mix together.

Arrange the lettuce, rocket, tomato, sliced chicken, noodles and boiled egg in 2 serving bowls and finish with the sauce. Top with daikon and chilli flakes.

Overleaf: Ramen Salad (left) and Creamy Chicken Ramen (right).

CREAMY CHICKEN RAMEN

Serves 2

The creaminess of tonkotsu pork ramen is legendary, but there is a growing trend for other creamy ramen as a filling alternative to the transparent broths. This chilled recipe is a refreshing but unctuous way to enjoy chicken and noodles.

~~~~~~

2 x 170 g (6 oz) chicken breast fillets
300 g (10½ oz) frozen fresh ramen
  noodles
½ head broccoli, cut into florets

SOYA-MISO CHILLED SOUP
170 ml (6 fl oz/¾ cup) unsweetened
  soya milk
1 tablespoon *mentsuyu* (Chinese soup
  stock), triple concentrated
2 teaspoons white miso powder
1–2 tablespoons ground white
  sesame seeds

TOPPINGS
Chilli Oil (*see page 30*)
Fresh flat-leaf parsley

Place the chicken in a saucepan and add lightly salted water to cover. Bring the pan to a boil. Once at a rolling boil, turn off the heat, cover with a lid and leave for 10 minutes. Remove the fillets, allow them to cool and cut into bite-size pieces.

For the soup, place the soya milk, *mentsuyu*, miso and ground sesame seeds in a bowl and mix well until the miso powder dissolves. Place in the refrigerator to chill.

Boil the noodles according to the instructions on the packet. Drain and plunge into iced water to firm them up. Steam the broccoli over boiling water for 3 minutes.

Divide the cold noodles between 2 serving bowls and pour over the chilled soup mixture. Top with the chicken and broccoli. Drizzle with the chilli oil and garnish with parsley.

TOFU & CHICKEN RAMEN

Serves 2

With the spicy chicken balanced with creamy egg and tofu, this delicious combination is a riot of taste and texture. For a vegan alternative, swap out the mince and egg for extra tofu and use vegan vegetable stock instead of chicken.

1 tablespoon sesame oil
1 tablespoon *tobanjan* (chilli bean paste)
1 clove garlic, grated
100 g (3½ oz) minced (ground) chicken
150 g (5¼ oz/1¾ cups) bean sprouts
500 ml (18 fl oz/2 cups) water
2 tablespoons *gochujang* (Korean red chilli paste)
1 tablespoon Japanese soy sauce
1½ teaspoons chicken stock powder, or 1 chicken stock (bouillon) cube
150 g (5¼ oz) firm tofu, cubed
1 egg, beaten
300 g (10½ oz) frozen fresh ramen noodles

TOPPINGS
1 tablespoon white sesame seeds
1–2 spring onions (scallions), sliced

Put the sesame oil, *tobanjan* and garlic in a frying pan and cook over a medium heat, taking care not to burn the garlic. Add the minced chicken and bean sprouts and stir until the meat is golden and cooked through.

Then pour over the water, *gochujang*, soy sauce and add the chicken stock powder. Mix well and bring to the boil. Add the tofu, bring back to a simmer and gently slip in the beaten egg, letting it float in the sauce.

Cook your noodles according to the instructions on the packet and divide between the 2 serving bowls. Top with the pork sauce and scatter the spring onions and sesame seeds over the top.

Toasting sesame seeds not only plumps the seeds but intensifies their nutty flavour. You can toast them on a baking sheet in the oven at medium heat for 8–10 minutes. If you are in a rush, though, raw sesame seeds work just as well as a ramen topping, adding extra texture and visual appeal.

CHICKEN CURRY RAMEN

Serves 2

Curry flavours arrived in Japan in the 1850s and are a modified version of the multiple spices used in traditional Indian curries. Still considered a Western favourite, curry became really popular in the 1960s and this recipe showcases how the Japanese have evolved their own delicious curry style.

2–3 medium carrots
1–2 spring onions (scallions)
240 g (8½ oz/2 nests) fresh Chinese noodles
1 tablespoon vegetable oil
150 g (5¼ oz) minced (ground) chicken
2 tablespoons frozen sweetcorn
Sea salt and freshly ground pepper
50 g (2 oz) medium-hot Japanese curry paste
1 teaspoon chicken stock powder
800 ml (28 fl oz/3⅓ cups) water

TOPPINGS
1 medium (US large) soft-boiled egg
1–2 spring onions (scallions), sliced
2 tablespoons canned sweetcorn

Peel the carrots and cut lengthways into thin ribbons. Slice the spring onions diagonally. Boil water in a saucepan, add the noodles, and cook according to the instructions on the packet. Drain well.

Heat the vegetable oil in a frying pan and add the minced chicken, carrots, spring onions and sweetcorn.

Stir-fry over a medium heat until the chicken changes colour. Season with salt and pepper, mixing everything together.

Now add the curry paste, chicken stock powder and water, and bring to the boil, stirring to combine. Reduce to a simmer and cook until the powder and paste dissolve.

Add the cooked noodles into the frying pan and stir everything through to coat with the curry sauce.

Divide between 2 serving bowls. Cut the soft-boiled egg in half and add one half to each bowl. Scatter over the spring onions and sweetcorn.

TOMATO & CHICKEN RAMEN

Serves 2

In the 1960s, Japan began importing ketchup from the USA, and, due to its high vinegar and sugar content, it became a popular replacement for such ingredients as tomato purée (paste). If you enjoy tomato-style pasta sauces, then try this tasty recipe.

2 x 170 g (6 oz) chicken breast fillets
240 g (8½ oz/2 nests) fresh Chinese
noodles
½ teaspoon granulated sugar
½ teaspoon salt
Freshly ground pepper
1 teaspoon Japanese soy sauce
2 teaspoons chicken stock powder
1 tablespoon tomato ketchup
400 ml (14 fl oz/1⅔ cups) unsalted
tomato juice
100 ml (3½ fl oz/scant ½ cup) water

TOPPINGS
2 tablespoons sesame oil
Shiso or spinach leaves, shredded

Boil plenty of water in a saucepan and add in the whole chicken breast fillets. Reduce the heat to low and poach for about 10 minutes, then remove the chicken and set aside. Bring back to the boil and scoop out any surface scum before adding the ramen and cooking over a medium heat for about 3 minutes. Once cooked, drain the noodles and snip them with scissors into easy-to-eat lengths. Shred the cooked chicken breast.

Put the sugar, salt, pepper, soy sauce, chicken stock powder, tomato ketchup, tomato juice and water in a pan and cook for 5–10 minutes over a medium heat, stirring until all the ingredients are blended well.

Serve the snipped noodles in the sauce, placing the chicken breast in a mound on top. Scatter over the shiso leaves and drizzle with sesame oil.

Shiso, or *oba*, leaves are often used in raw fish dishes in Japan, as traditionally they were thought to be an intestine aid and to protect against food poisoning. With an elegant, unique flavour, akin to aniseed, and a strong aroma, they add a refreshing accent to salads and noodle dishes.

CHICKEN WING RAMEN

Serves 2

This recipe marinates chicken wings in oyster sauce. Made from sugar, salt and oyster extracts, the condiment has traditionally been used in Cantonese cooking, as oysters were plentiful off the shores of Hong Kong and Guandong. It is said to have been invented by Lee Kum Sheung, a restaurateur in southern China, in 1888.

6 whole chicken wings, weighing 600 g (1 lb 5 oz) in total
800 ml (28 fl oz/3⅓ cups) water
2 teaspoons chicken stock powder
2 tablespoons cooking saké
4 teaspoons Japanese soy sauce
½ teaspoon sesame oil
1 tablespoon vegetable oil
4 bulbs pak choi (bok choy)
300 g (10½ oz) frozen fresh ramen noodles

MARINADE
2 teaspoons granulated sugar
2 tablespoons Japanese soy sauce
2 tablespoons cooking saké
2 tablespoons oyster sauce

TOPPINGS
1–2 spring onions (scallions), sliced
Chilli flakes

Break the wings in two at the joint. Cut a line along the meatier end to help the cooking process. Place the chicken wing tip pieces in a pot, cover with the water and add the chicken stock powder, saké, soy sauce and sesame oil. Simmer over medium heat for 10–15 minutes while skimming off the scum. Strain to create the broth and discard the tips.

Make the marinade. Combine the sugar, soy sauce, saké and oyster sauce in a bowl. Dip the remaining chicken wing pieces in the marinade, toss to coat and leave for about 10 minutes.

Heat the vegetable oil in a frying pan and add the marinated chicken wings. Brown all over, draining any juices and excess fat when cooked. Add the remaining marinade sauce, cover with a lid and simmer over a low heat for 2–3 minutes.

Trim the base from the pak choi and cut the stalks (stems) into quarters lengthways. Blanche for 1–2 minutes in boiling salted water, then drain.

Cook the noodles in boiling water according to the instructions on the packet. Drain and divide between the serving bowls before pouring over the broth. Add in the wings and sauce. Top with the pak choi and finish with spring onions and chilli flakes.

TAN TAN MEN

Serves 2

This Japanese version of a traditional Sichuan ramen features
aromatic, fried chicken in a spicy tahini-flavoured creamy
broth for a one-stop meal in a bowl.

2 cloves garlic
1 tablespoon vegetable oil
2 tablespoons Japanese soy sauce
2 tablespoons oyster sauce
200 g (7 oz) minced (ground) chicken
150 ml (5 fl oz/⅔ cup) water
2 teaspoons chicken stock powder,
    or 1 chicken stock (bouillon) cube
200 ml (7 fl oz/scant 1 cup) almond or
    soya milk
240 g (8½ oz/2 nests) fresh Chinese
    noodles

TAHINI SAUCE
1–3 teaspoons Chilli Oil (*see page 30*),
    to taste
1 tablespoon Japanese soy sauce
1 tablespoon tahini

TOPPINGS
1–2 spring onions (scallions), sliced
2 Soy-marinated Eggs (*see page 37*)
Fresh spinach leaves

Finely mince the garlic. Heat the vegetable oil in a frying pan over a
medium-high heat, add the garlic and fry until lightly golden. Add the
soy sauce and oyster sauce and stir well for about 1 minute. Then add
in the minced chicken and cook for a further 5-6 minutes until the
chicken is cooked through and browned.

For the soup, place the water in a pot over a medium-high heat, then add
the chicken stock and almond or soya milk. Do not allow to boil, but just
gently simmer. Meanwhile cook your ramen noodles according to the
instructions on the packet. Make the tahini sauce by mixing the chilli oil,
soy sauce and tahini in a small bowl until combined.

Divide the noodles between 2 bowls, mix in the soup and sauce, spoon
the chicken on top, and add the halved eggs, spinach and spring onion.

Pronounced in Chinese as *dan dan*, the name of this
dish refers to the shoulder pole used to transport baskets
of the flavoured oil and chicken noodle dish to sell to
hungry customers around Chengdu. Originally a soup-
less noodle dish, to make carrying it easier, the modern
version contains a broth element.

SWEET & SPICY DUCK RAMEN

Serves 2

The rich taste and luxurious texture of duck makes it a great ingredient
to team with other bold flavours. This recipe will have your taste buds
singing with the saccharine depth of teriyaki and deep heat of *gochujang*.

~~~~~~

240 g (8½ oz) duck breast
2 tablespoons vegetable oil
800 ml (28 fl oz/3⅓ cups) water
1 tablespoon chicken stock powder
1 tablespoon *nam pla* (fish sauce)
1 tablespoon chilli sauce, such as sriracha
2 teaspoons Japanese soy sauce
240 g (8½ oz/2 nests) fresh Chinese
    noodles

MARINADE
4 tablespoons teriyaki sauce
1 tablespoon *gochujang* (Korean red
    chilli paste)
1 tablespoon mirin
1 tablespoon cooking saké

TOPPINGS
1 fresh red bird's-eye chilli, deseeded and
    finely sliced on the diagonal
75 g (2½ oz) shallots, finely chopped
Chinese chives, chopped

Make the marinade. Mix the teriyaki sauce, *gochujang*, mirin and saké
in a bowl. Add the duck breast, making sure you coat both sides with
the marinade. Cover and refrigerate for a minimum of 20 minutes.

Preheat the oven to 180°C (350°F/Gas mark 4).

Place an ovenproof pan over a medium heat and add the vegetable oil.
Once the oil is hot, fry the duck for 3 minutes on each side. Transfer to
the preheated oven for 7 minutes for medium rare. Remove the duck
from the oven and set aside to cool to room temperature.

Place the water in a large pot over a high heat, add the chicken stock
powder, fish sauce, chilli sauce and soy sauce, and simmer for 3 minutes.

Cook the noodles according to the instructions on the packet. Drain
and divide between 2 serving bowls. Pour over the broth.

The duck should now be cool to the touch. Slice it thinly and arrange
the duck slices on top of the noodles and broth. Scatter over the sliced
red chilli, shallots and chives.

Overleaf: Tan Tan Men (left) and Sweet & Spicy Duck Ramen (right).

YUZU DUCK RAMEN

Serves 2

Duck is a much-favoured ingredient in Chinese cuisine, however,
it also eaten in Japan in a style called *yakatori* – a pan-roasted,
marinated dish. This recipe fuses duck's richness with the
refreshing, fragrant citrus hit of yuzu.

2 skin-on duck breasts, weighing
   200 g (7 oz) each
2 teaspoons coarse sea salt
2 teaspoons ground coriander
400 ml (14 fl oz/1⅔ cups) water
2 tablespoons cooking saké
2 tablespoons light soy sauce
1 teaspoon chicken stock powder
½ teaspoon kelp (kombu) stock powder
240 g (8½ oz/2 nests) fresh Chinese
   noodles

TOPPINGS
3–4 slivers fresh yuzu
1–2 teaspoons *yuzu kosho*
Spring onions (scallions), sliced

Heat the oven on to 200°C (400°F/Gas mark 6).

Use a clean, sharp knife to make shallow cuts in the skin of the duck breasts. Make 5 cuts in one direction across the width of the skin, then rotate 90 degrees and make 5 more cuts to create a cross pattern. This will help release the fat from the skin as the duck cooks. You do not want to penetrate the meat, so try not to apply too much pressure when making the cuts.

Scatter the salt and coriander over the duck skin, then place them, skin-side down, in a cold, large ovenproof pan and cook over a medium heat for 5 minutes. When the pan begins to spit fat vigorously, reduce the heat slightly. Flip the breasts and cook for another 2 minutes.

Now place the pan in the oven for 5 minutes for medium rare. If you want the meat to cook well, leave it in the oven for a few minutes more. Transfer to a chopping board and allow it to rest for 5 minutes.

Don't throw the oil away! Keep it in the pan. While the duck is resting, add the water to the pan and bring to the boil. Add the saké, light soy sauce, chicken stock powder and kelp stock powder, and simmer.

Cook the fresh noodles in boiling water for 3 minutes. Drain and divide between 2 serving bowls. Spoon over the hot soup. Slice the duck thinly and arrange on top of the bowls. Top with sliced yuzu, *yuzu kosho* and scatter over the spring onions.

DUCK DIPPING RAMEN

Serves 2

Ramen pioneer Kazuo Yamagishi is credited with creating dipping noodles, called *tsukemen*, in the 1950s. It is a way of serving noodles and soup in separate bowls to be enjoyed together by dipping one into the other. This allows the noodles to be enjoyed cooler than they would be in a broth; they can even be served cold.

1 medium white onion
6 spring onions (scallions)
200 g (7 oz) skin-on duck breast
240 g (8½ oz/2 nests) fresh Chinese noodles
300 ml (10 fl oz/1¼ cups) water
2 teaspoons kelp (kombu) stock powder
2 tablespoons Japanese soy sauce
2 tablespoons cooking saké
50 ml (1¾ fl oz/scant ¼ cup) mirin

TOPPING
1 teaspoon *shichimi togarashi*, to taste

Slice the onion into 1 cm (½ in) semicircles and slice the spring onions thinly. Slice the duck breast into thin strips. Cook the ramen noodles in boiling water according to the instructions on the packet. Drain and rinse in cold water.

Add the water, kelp stock powder, soy sauce, saké and mirin to a saucepan over a high heat, stir and bring to the boil. Once it is boiling, drop in the onion slices then reduce heat and simmer gently.

Place a frying pan over a medium-high heat and stir-fry the duck strips and spring onions quickly for about 5 minutes to lock in the flavour and texture. Be careful not to overcook the duck meat.

Once done, stir the duck and spring onions into the broth base.

Divide the cool noodles between 2 serving bowls. Pour the duck soup into 2 other bowls, ready to dip. Scatter over the *shichimi togarashi*.

To eat, use chopsticks to dip some of the cooled noodles into the hot duck dipping broth and slurp up.

3
PORK & BEEF RAMEN

While Wagyu and Kobe beef have become world renowned for their melt-in-the-mouth, marbled appeal, more affordable cuts of beef make an accessible centrepiece for a delicious bowl of ramen. Japan's most popular meat, however, is pork, as it takes on flavours beautifully and adds texture, whether minced (ground) and fried with aromatic flavourings or as an unctuous slice of pork belly laid across the top of a noodle bowl.

PORK CHASHU RAMEN

Serves 2

The Cantonese style of cooking pork was originally a barbecued version called *char siu*, meaning 'fork-roasted'. In this dish, the pork belly is fried over a high heat in a dry pan to give it that charred quality. Slices of tender pork belly, cooked in a sweet and salty sauce, make a delicious ramen topping for a satisfying meal.

450 g (1 lb) pork belly
3 tablespoons cooking saké
1 litre (35 fl oz/4¼ cups) water plus
    600 ml (20 fl oz/2½ cups)
1 clove garlic, thinly sliced
1 teaspoon grated fresh ginger root
3 tablespoons Japanese soy sauce
3 tablespoons honey
1 tablespoon oyster sauce
240 g (8½ oz/2 nests) fresh Chinese
    noodles

TOPPINGS
Soy-marinated Egg (*see page 37*)
3 spring onions (scallions), green part cut
    into 5 cm (2 in) lengths

Pierce the pork belly all over with a fork. Place in a deep hot frying pan over a medium heat and brown the surface. Add the saké and 1 litre (35 fl oz/4¼ cups) water and turn the heat to high. Bring to the boil, then reduce the heat to low, cover and simmer for 30 minutes.

When ready, remove from the heat and set aside about 100 ml (3½ fl oz/scant ½ cup) of the cooking liquid, discarding the rest. In a separate saucepan, add the garlic, grated ginger, soy sauce, honey, oyster sauce and reserved cooking liquid and bring it to the boil.

Place the pork belly back in the pan for 2 minutes before removing it and carving the belly into thin slices. Allow the pork slices to rest.

Meanwhile simmer any remaining meat juices in the pan for about 10 minutes until reduced to make the broth sauce. Boil the 600 ml (20 fl oz/2½ cups) of water, and divide between 2 serving bowls. Add the reduced sauce to the water and twirl it through with chopsticks or a fork to blend.

Cook the noodles according to the instructions on the packet. Drain and divide the noodles between the 2 bowls. Top with the pork belly slices and add a halved egg to each bowl. Scatter over the spring onions.

KIMCHI RAMEN

Serves 2

Known as 'Korean pickles', it wasn't until the 1980s that kimchi started to become more commonplace in Japanese cuisine, though it was consumed by the Korean immigrant population. In this recipe, there is little broth, as the sauce simply coats the noodles.

~~~~~~

800 g (10½ oz/1 lb 12 oz) frozen fresh ramen
150 g (5¼ oz) minced (ground) pork
80 g (3 oz/⅓ cup) kimchi
2 tablespoons Korean BBQ sauce (any brand of your preference)
2 tablespoons *mentsuyu* (Chinese soup stock), double concentrated
2 tablespoons sesame oil

TOPPINGS
Black sesame seeds
2 egg yolks
Extra kimchi (optional)

Boil the ramen noodles according to the instructions on the packet, then drain and set aside.

Next bring a saucepan of water to the boil and add your minced pork, cooking it for 3 minutes before draining through a sieve.

Divide the pork and kimchi between 2 serving bowls and mix well. Add 1 tablespoon each of the Korean BBQ sauce, *mentsuyu* and sesame oil to each bowl, and mix again.

Toss in the cooked noodles to coat, then scatter over black sesame seeds and top with an egg yolk and extra kimchi, if desired.

~~~~~~

Kimchi, the fiery fermented cabbage, is a traditional Korean dish that originated over 3,000 years ago as a way to preserve vegetables during cold winters. Sour and tangy, it is eaten as a side dish with almost every meal in South Korea.

NARUTO RAMEN

Serves 2

This nourishing ramen is inspired by the favourite
dish of the popular Japanese manga character Naruto.
Nothing warms Naruto's heart more than a bowl of
ramen with an extra roasted pork topping. The ginger,
mirin and miso flavours of this dish will warm yours.

300 g (10½ oz) frozen fresh ramen
  noodles
1½ teaspoons sesame oil
1 tablespoon garlic purée
1 teaspoon ginger purée
2 tablespoons white miso paste
1 tablespoon mirin
1½ teaspoons Japanese soy sauce
2–3 tablespoons chicken stock powder,
  or 2 chicken stock (bouillon) cubes
500 ml (18 fl oz/2 cups) water
200 g (7 oz) roasted pork slices (shop-
  bought)
300 g (10½ oz/3 cups) bean sprouts
250–300 ml (9–10 fl oz/1⅓ cup) soya milk
1 tablespoon ground sesame seeds
Freshly ground black pepper

TOPPINGS
6 slices *narutomaki* (fishcake)
2 Spice-seasoned Eggs (*see page 37*)
Menma (fermented bamboo shoots)
1–2 spring onions (scallions), sliced
Nori sheets and *shichimi togarashi*

Prepare your ramen noodles according to the instructions on the packet.
Drain and set aside.

Place the sesame oil, garlic purée, ginger purée, miso, mirin, soy sauce,
chicken stock powder and water into a saucepan and bring to the boil.
Add the pork slices and, after 1 minute or so, the bean sprouts.

When the bean sprouts are softened, after 2–3 minutes, add in the soya
milk, being careful not to bring the broth to the boil. Once heated through,
stir in the ground sesame seeds and a little black pepper to taste.

Divide the noodles between 2 bowls, pour over the pork and soup, and
top each with 3 slices of *narutomaki* and a halved egg. Add spring onions,
menma, the nori and a scattering of *shichimi*.

Cut sheets of nori to size and add to your ramen bowl.
The salty seaweed is paper thin and delicious, but eat
it quickly as it will get soggy in the broth.

FLUFFY EGG RAMEN

Serves 2

In this nourishing recipe, freshly beaten egg is stirred straight into the broth. It creates a delicious texture and adds richness to the dish. Serve over noodles for an easy, lazy supper.

~~~~~~

200 g (7 oz) sliced pork belly
6 Chinese chives
½ large carrot
2 teaspoons sesame oil
800 ml (28 fl oz/3⅓ cups) water
2–3 tablespoons chicken stock powder, or
    2 chicken stock (bouillon) cubes
1 tablespoon Japanese soy sauce
1 tablespoon mirin
100 g (3½ oz/1 cup) bean sprouts
2 medium (US large) eggs, beaten
240 g (8½ oz/2 nests) fresh Chinese
    noodles

TOPPINGS
2 teaspoons sesame seeds
Mayu (black garlic oil)

Cut the pork belly strips and the chives into 3 cm (1¼ in) lengths. Finely chop the carrot.

Heat the sesame oil in a pot over medium heat and fry off the pork and carrots. When the pork changes colour, add the water, chicken stock, soy sauce and mirin. Simmer for 3-4 minutes until the carrots are soft.

Add the chives and bean sprouts and bring to the boil. Add the beaten egg to the pot, turning off the heat when the egg becomes fluffy.

Cook the noodles following the instructions on the packet, drain and divide between 2 serving bowls. Pour over the pork belly broth and scatter with sesame seeds. Add a few drops of black garlic oil.

~~~~~~

When adding eggs directly to a broth, it is vital to beat the egg before adding it into boiling liquid. You can, however, crack a whole egg into the broth to poach it, but you will need to reduce the boiling broth to a simmer first, then continue to baste it with spoonfuls of hot broth until it is cooked to your liking.

ADDICTIVE ONE-POT RAMEN

Serves 2

These moreish noodles with charred crispy pork
belly are packed with flavour and irresistible. The
yuzu adds a refreshing, citrus flavour.

1 tablespoon sesame oil
200 g (7 oz) pork belly, thinly sliced
3–4 spring onions (scallions)
Sea salt
600 ml (20 fl oz/2½ cups) water
2 tablespoons *mentsuyu* (Chinese soup
  stock), double concentrated, diluted
  with 6 tablespoons water
8 g (¼ oz/ 2½ teaspoons) kelp (kombu)
  stock powder
2 teaspoons granulated sugar
1 tablespoon yuzu purée
300 g (10½ oz/2 nests) frozen
  fresh ramen noodles

TOPPINGS
Yuzu zest strips
Shredded nori

Coat a frying pan with the sesame oil, then place the pork belly strips
and spring onions in the pan with a pinch of salt.

Fry over a high heat until the belly is crispy and the spring onions are
lightly charred. Then add the water, *mentsuyu*, kelp stock powder, sugar
and yuzu purée. Reduce to a medium heat and cook for 5–7 minutes. As
the broth warms, add the noodles and cook them directly in the sauce
for 2 minutes until cooked.

Divide the pork belly, noodles and sauce mixture into 2 serving bowls.
Top with shredded nori and yuzu zest for texture and a citrus tang.

The yellow yuzu fruit is a popular souring agent in
Japan, adding a tang of citrus to dishes. Both the zest
and juices can be used and it is more fragrant than its
lemon and lime counterparts.

Overleaf: Fluffy Egg Ramen (left) and Addictive One-Pot Ramen (right).

HEARTY PORK MINCE BROTH

Serves 2

This intensely flavoured and warming broth is more stew-like
than other dashi broths as it includes soybean paste, shiitake
mushrooms and potato starch. It makes generous portions.

1 clove garlic
5 cm (2 in) fresh ginger root
5 spring onions (scallions)
40 g (1½ oz) shiitake mushrooms
40 g (1½ oz/⅓ cup) tinned bamboo
    shoots
1 tablespoon vegetable oil
160 g (5½ oz) minced (ground) pork
1 teaspoon *doenjang* (soybean paste)
25 ml (1 fl oz/5 teaspoons) sweet
    soy sauce
4 tablespoons cooking saké
2 tablespoons mirin
1 tablespoon Japanese soy sauce
1 tablespoon Chicken Dashi
    (*see page 26*)
500 ml (18 fl oz/2 cups) water
1 tablespoon potato starch, dissolved
    in 3 tablespoons water
240 g (8½ oz/2 nests) fresh Chinese
    noodles

TOPPINGS
1 tablespoon sesame oil
40 g (1½ oz) cucumber, julienned

Finely chop the garlic, ginger, spring onions, shiitake mushrooms and
bamboo shoots.

Lightly oil a frying pan with the vegetable oil and stir-fry the garlic
and ginger for about 2 minutes until fragrant. Add the minced pork and
stir-fry until the moisture has evaporated. Add in the *doenjang* and sweet
soy sauce and stir-fry until nearly dry. Then add the saké, mirin, soy
sauce, chicken dashi and water. Simmer over a medium heat for about
5 minutes. When the water level is low, slowly add the water-soluble
potato starch until the broth thickens.

Prepare your noodles according to the instructions on the packet. Drain
and divide between the 2 serving bowls. Pour over the pork sauce and
top with the cucumber. Drizzle with sesame oil to finish.

Doenjang is a Korean spicy paste made from
fermented soybeans and brine. It has an umami, salty
flavour profile and can be used to season broths. The
paste is usually stir-fried in oil to release its intense
depth of flavour.

THICK MISO RAMEN

Serves 2

The *tobanjan* adds heat to this ramen dish, while the Shantung soup seasoning, a paste-like Chinese soup mixture of oils, onions, garlic and spices, gives a delicate, sweet, umami flavour to the broth.

1 tablespoon sesame oil
80 g (3 oz) minced (ground) pork
1 clove garlic, grated
4 cm (1½ in) fresh ginger, grated
1 teaspoon *tobanjan* (chilli bean paste)
1 tablespoon grated carrot
3 tablespoons grated white onion
1 teaspoon grated celery
4 tablespoons unsweetened miso paste
1 teaspoon Shantung soup seasoning
1 teaspoon granulated sugar
2 teaspoons Japanese soy sauce
700 ml (24 fl oz/3 cups) water
240 g (8½ oz/2 nests) fresh Chinese noodles

TOPPINGS

1–2 spring onions (scallions), sliced
1 medium (US large) boiled egg, halved
Aromatic Oil (*see page 30*)

Heat the sesame oil in a large frying pan and fry the minced pork. Add the garlic, ginger and *tobanjan* and stir-fry for 5–10 minutes.

Add the grated carrot, onion and celery to the pan, along with the miso paste, Shantung soup seasoning and sugar. Stir-fry for about 5 minutes until the vegetables are tender. Sprinkle in the soy sauce and continue to stir-fry for another minute or so, then add in the water and bring to the boil.

In another saucepan, bring water to the boil and cook the Chinese noodles according to the instructions on the packet. Drain well and place in 2 serving bowls. Pour the hot soup into the bowls, top with spring onions and half a boiled egg, and add a dash of the aromatic oil to flavour.

Tobanjan is a Sichuan-style paste made from broad beans and a special blend of chillies. Although it isn't overly spicy, it is a great ingredient to use as a dipping sauce or for adding a little heat to broths and stir-fried meats and vegetables.

TAIWAN RAMEN

Serves 2

The name for this well-known dish is a little misleading as the recipe isn't from Taiwan but from Nagoya, Japan. The dish was created in the 1980s when a love of spicy food started to boom.

~~~~~~

2–3 dried whole red chillies
2 cloves garlic
5 cm (2 in) fresh ginger root
100 g (3½ oz/1 cup) bean sprouts
1 tablespoon sesame oil
1 teaspoon *tobanjan* (chilli bean paste)
200 g (7 oz) minced (ground) pork
2 teaspoons chicken stock powder
2 teaspoons Japanese soy sauce
Sea salt and ground black pepper
1 litre (35 fl oz/4¼ cups) water
280 g (10 oz) Chinese
    glass noodles

TOPPINGS

Chinese chives, cut into
    5 cm (2 in) lengths
Purple daikon (mooli), sliced

Remove the seeds from the dried red chilli and slice thinly.

Very finely chop the garlic and ginger, and rinse the bean sprouts under cold running water. Heat the sesame oil in a frying pan and fry the garlic and ginger for about 2 minutes until fragrant. Add the *tobanjan* and stir-fry for 1 minute more, then add the red dried chilli and minced pork and fry until crispy.

Once cooked through, add the chicken stock powder and soy sauce, lightly season with salt and pepper, and continue frying for another minute.

Pour the water over the mixture and simmer for 4–5 minutes, then add the bean sprouts. Put the noodles directly into the broth and allow them to cook through according to the instructions on the packet.

Divide the soup between 2 serving bowls, then top with the chives and sliced radish.

WONTON RAMEN

Serves 2

This traditional favourite has its origins in China and Canton where the word *wonton* means 'swallowing cloud'. For this recipe, we are creating our own dumplings, but you could easily use frozen shop-bought ones for a quick treat.

4 spring onions (scallions)
2 teaspoons sesame oil
100 g (3½ oz) minced (ground) pork
1 teaspoon kelp (kombu) stock powder
8 wonton wrappers (skins)
240 g (8½ oz/2 nests) fresh Chinese noodles
800 ml (28 fl oz/3⅓ cups) water
1 tablespoon chicken stock powder, or 1 chicken stock (bouillon) cube
2 teaspoons Japanese soy sauce
2 teaspoons mirin

TOPPINGS
Grated fresh ginger root
Chinese chives, chopped
Sesame oil

Chop the spring onions into small pieces. Heat the sesame oil in a frying pan and add the spring onions and minced pork. Sprinkle in the kelp powder. Stir-fry for 3–4 minutes until the meat is cooked through. Remove from the pan and set aside. Allow to cool slightly.

To fill a wonton, lay a wrapper on a flat working surface. Place 2 teaspoons of pork filling in the centre of the square, then fold the wrapper in half from corner to corner, creating a triangle. Pat lightly around the filling to get rid of any air pockets and press the edges to seal. Dab one of the bottom corners of the triangle with a little water. Now, holding the bottom corners of the triangle, bring those two corners together to join and squeeze to seal. This creates a bonnet shape. Repeat with the other wonton wrappers.

Meanwhile make the noodles by cooking them according to the instructions on the packet. Drain and divide between 2 serving bowls.

Add the water, chicken stock, soy sauce and mirin to a saucepan. Bring to a light boil, stirring constantly. Once bubbling, gently drop in the wonton dumplings and let them simmer for 2 minutes. Pour over the noodles, top with the ginger and chives and drizzle with sesame oil.

CHANPON

Serves 2

Chanpon is a famed regional dish. Originally from Nagasaki, Japan, it became a go-to recipe, due to its affordable and filling ingredients and luxuriant broth.

150 g (5¼ oz) pork belly, thinly sliced
70 g (2½ oz) *narutomaki* or *kamaboko* (fishcake)
1½ teaspoons sesame oil
200 g (7 oz/1½–2 cups) trimmed vegetables, such as carrot slices, green beans, broccoli, mangetout (snow peas), baby sweetcorn; alternatively, pre-cut stir-fry vegetables
1 tablespoon saké
⅜ teaspoon salt
1½ teaspoons granulated sugar
1 teaspoon oyster sauce
1½ teaspoons chicken glass noodle soup base
400 ml (14 fl oz/1⅔ cups) water
100 ml (3½ fl oz/scant ½ cup) full-fat (whole) milk
300 g (5¼ oz/2 nests) frozen fresh ramen

TOPPING
1–2 tablespoons tinned sweetcorn

Cut the sliced belly pork into bite-sized pieces. Cut the *narutomaki* into thin slices.

Heat the sesame oil in a deep frying pan, add the pork and fry over a medium heat until it changes colour. Add the trimmed vegetables and stir-fry quickly for 4–5 minutes until soft to the bite. Then add the saké, salt, sugar, oyster sauce, chicken glass noodle soup base and water. Mix well and bring to the boil.

Add the Chinese noodles and boil for about 2 minutes, loosening the noodles as they cook. Then lightly drop in the slices of *narutomaki* and pour in the milk. Ensure the broth is warmed through.

Divide the chanpon between 2 deep serving bowls and scatter over the sweetcorn.

Chicken glass noodle soup base comes in a powder form, like other dried stocks, making it easy to dissolve into broths. You can substitute your preferred chicken stock powder or cube if you prefer.

COCONUT CURRY RAMEN

Serves 2

This recipe plays on the comforting and fragrant flavours
of coconut. The gently sweet coconut milk, fresh coriander
(cilantro) and zingy ginger make a gorgeously aromatic dish.

1 teaspoon sesame oil
1 tablespoon *nam pla* (fish sauce)
2 teaspoons oyster sauce
1 tablespoon curry powder
100 g (3½ oz) minced (ground) pork
1 medium white onion, thinly sliced
½ teaspoon grated fresh ginger root
½ teaspoon grated garlic
400 ml (14 fl oz/1⅔ cups) coconut milk
100 ml (3½ fl oz/scant ½ cup) water
300 g (10½ oz) frozen fresh ramen
    noodles

TOPPINGS
6 cherry tomatoes, halved
Grated fresh ginger root
1 bunch fresh coriander (cilantro)
    leaves, chopped
Furikake

Heat the sesame oil in a frying pan, add the fish sauce, oyster sauce and curry powder, and fry over a medium heat for 1 minute. Next, add in the minced pork and continue to fry until the meat changes colour.

Add the onion slices, ginger and garlic, and stir-fry for another 3–4 minutes, before pouring in the coconut milk and water. Bring the curry to a boil. When it boils, place the noodles into the sauce. Cook according to the timings on the packet, loosening the noodles in the sauce as they cook.

Divide the ramen curry between 2 serving bowls and top with the cherry tomatoes, grated ginger and coriander. Scatter over the *furikake*.

Coconut isn't an overly used ingredient in Japan, but the Meiji era (1868–1912) saw more Westernized foods gaining favour. Dishes like katsu curry, which uses coconut milk, started to become increasingly popular. You can also find coconut used in *dango*, a Japanese sweet dumpling made with mochi flour.

SPICY KOREAN RAMEN

Serves 2

Korean-inspired noodle dishes are high in flavour intensity with the addition of *gochujang*, a fermented chilli paste. In Korea, noodles have always been considered an affordable staple, while rice was an ingredient reserved for the more prosperous. Korea is a hub for instant noodles and has made the already popular noodle even more widespread.

½ large carrot

2 shiitake mushrooms

½ medium white onion

250 g (8¾ oz/8 cups) spinach

1 clove garlic

1 tablespoon sesame oil for frying plus extra 1 teaspoon for the broth

150 g (5¼ oz) minced (ground) pork

2 tablespoons ground sesame seeds

½ teaspoon salt

240 g (8½ oz) fresh Chinese noodles

600 ml (20 fl oz/3⅓ cups) water

1½ tablespoons *gochujang* (Korean red chilli paste)

2 teaspoons chicken stock powder

2 tablespoons of cooking saké

4 teaspoons of soy sauce

TOPPINGS

2 medium (US large) soft-boiled eggs

½ fresh red chilli pepper, finely sliced

2 teaspoons white sesame seeds

Finely slice the carrot, shiitake mushrooms, onion and spinach. Finely chop the garlic.

Add the sesame oil to a frying pan and stir-fry the garlic and minced pork for 4–5 minutes until the colour changes. Add in the vegetables in order of cooking times – first the carrots and onions, then the mushrooms and finally the spinach – stir-frying for a total of 4–5 minutes until the carrots are softened but still retain some bite. Sprinkle over the ground sesame seeds and salt and fry for a further minute to release the flavours. Now turn off the heat and set aside.

To make the broth, put the *gochujang*, chicken stock powder, saké, soy sauce and 1 teaspoon sesame oil into a pan with the water, mix well and bring to a fast simmer.

Cook the noodles according to the instructions on the packet, then divide between 2 bowls, pour over the broth and top with the stir-fried vegetables. Add a soft-boiled egg, halved, to each and scatter over red chilli slices and white sesame seeds.

SUPER SPICY NOODLES

Serves 2

If you are a serious heat-seeker, this recipe is guaranteed to satisfy your spice cravings. Adjust the amount of chilli flavour to your liking.

2 cloves garlic
4–5 spring onions (scallions)
200 g (7 oz) pork belly, thinly sliced
Sea salt and ground black pepper
2 tablespoons sesame oil
1 x 200 gram (7 oz) tin chopped tomatoes
600 ml (20 fl oz/2½ cups) water
2 tablespoons chicken stock powder
1 teaspoon *mentsuyu* (Chinese soup stock), triple concentrated
1 tablespoon oyster sauce
1 tablespoon chilli pepper flakes
2 teaspoons granulated sugar
300 g (10½ oz/2 nests) fresh Chinese noodles

TOPPINGS
Chilli Oil (*see page 30*)
1 tablespoon white or black sesame seeds

Finely chop the garlic and slice the spring onions diagonally. Season the pork belly with salt and pepper.

Add the sesame oil to a frying pan over a medium heat, then add the garlic, spring onions and pork. Stir-fry for 5–7 minutes until the pork becomes crispy.

Pour in the chopped tomatoes and simmer for another 5 minutes until the juice is completely evaporated. Next add the water, chicken stock powder, *mentsuyu*, oyster sauce, chilli pepper flakes and sugar. Bring the mixture to the boil, stirring gently.

When it is boiling, add the Chinese noodles directly to the pan and cook for the time instructed on the packet. Divide between 2 serving bowls and top with the chilli oil and sesame seeds.

Togarashi is the Japanese name given to the hot red South American pepper used to make chilli flakes. It's also the ingredient that makes *shichimi* so spicy.

TAHINI RAMEN

Serves 2

This recipe incorporates the creamy, oily, richness of tahini.
Look out for *neri goma*, or 'kneaded sesame', which is a
Japanese sesame paste similar to the Middle Eastern tahini.

1 clove garlic
3 cm (1¼ in) fresh ginger root
1 tablespoon vegetable oil
200 g (7 oz) minced (ground) pork
Sea salt and ground black pepper
5 tablespoons tahini
2 tablespoons Japanese soy sauce
600 ml (20 fl oz/2½ cups) water
1 tablespoon white miso paste
1 tablespoon chicken stock powder
1 teaspoon *tobanjan* (chilli bean paste)
240 g (8½ oz /2 nests) fresh Chinese
  noodles

TOPPINGS
1–2 spring onions (scallions), sliced
Chilli Oil (*see page 30*)

Grate the garlic and peel and grate the ginger root.

Heat the vegetable oil in a frying pan over a medium-high heat and stir in the garlic and ginger. When they are fragrant, after about 2 minutes, add the minced pork, season with salt and pepper, and fry for 4–5 minutes more until the meat becomes grey and is fully cooked.

Add the tahini, soy sauce, water, miso paste, chicken stock powder and *tobanjan* to the pan. Bring the soup mixture to a soft boil, stirring lightly.

Meanwhile prepare the noodles according to the instructions on the packet. Drain and divide between 2 serving bowls.

Pour over the warm pork soup and scatter over spring onions. Drizzle with the chilli oil to finish.

Authentic Japanese sesame sauce, *goma dare*, differs slightly from its Middle Eastern counterpart (tahini) in that the sesame seeds are roasted or toasted rather than raw. It is also slightly runnier in texture, making it a delicious dipping sauce.

JAJA RAMEN

Serves 2

Salty and savoury, this Chinese–Korean-inspired bowl
of ramen makes a great supper dish for two. From *jajamen*,
which means 'fried sauce noodles', the dish is less brothy
than many other ramen recipes.

14 dried shiitake mushrooms, rehydrated
1 large leek, using only 10 cm (4 in) of the
    white bulb
1 tablespoon sesame oil plus ½ teaspoon
1 tablespoon finely chopped garlic
1 tablespoon finely chopped fresh
    ginger root
150 g (5¼ oz) minced (ground) pork
1 teaspoon *gochujang* (Korean red
    chilli paste)
600 ml (20 fl oz/2½ cups) water
2 teaspoons chicken stock powder
2 tablespoons cooking saké
4 teaspoons soy sauce
Sea salt and ground black pepper
    (optional)
240 g (8½ oz/2 nests) fresh Chinese
    noodles
Sea salt and ground black pepper

TOPPING
Cucumber, julienned

Finely chop the dried, rehydrated mushrooms. Slice the leek finely.

Heat the 1 tablespoon of sesame oil in a frying pan over a low heat
and add the garlic and ginger for 1–2 minutes until fragrant. Add in
the mushrooms and leek and continue to fry over low heat for about
2 minutes more. Add the minced pork and *gochujang* to the pan,
increase the heat to medium, and stir continuously to cook evenly.

Once the meat is cooked, after about 4 minutes, add in the water, chicken
stock powder, saké, soy sauce and ½ teaspoon of sesame oil and bring to a
simmer. Stir lightly over a low heat for another minute or so. If you need to,
season with a pinch of salt and pepper.

Cook the noodles in separate pan of boiling water according to the
instructions on the packet.

Drain the noodles, toss with a few drops of sesame oil and divide
between 2 serving bowls. Top with the pork, mushroom and sauce mix.
Finish with cucumber.

CARBONARA RAMEN

Serves 2

Surprise friends with a ramen twist on this classic
Italian favourite. An unconventional but fun and tasty
recipe, the addition of spinach and an egg yolk bring
the bowl to life with colour and texture.

~~~~~~

4 rashers (slices) streaky bacon
100 g (3½ oz/3½ cups) fresh spinach
1 teaspoon olive oil
Salt and ground black pepper
200 ml (7 fl oz/scant 1 cup) milk
800 ml (28 fl oz/3⅓ cups) water
2 teaspoons chicken stock powder
2 tablespoons of cooking saké
4 teaspoons of soy sauce
½ teaspoon sesame oil
240 g (8½ oz/2 nests) fresh Chinese
   noodles

TOPPINGS
2 raw egg yolks
40 g (1½ oz /⅓ cup) grated
   Cheddar cheese
Freshly ground black pepper
1 tablespoon olive oil

Slice the bacon into 1 cm (½ in) pieces. Remove the stalk (stem) ends of the spinach leaves, cut a cross at the stalks, then cut into bite-sized strips.

Heat the olive oil in a frying pan over a medium heat, add the bacon and fry lightly. After about 4–5 minutes, when golden, add the spinach and fry until tender. Season to taste, remove from the heat and set aside.

Place the milk, water, chicken stock powder, saké, soy sauce and sesame oil in a pan and bring to a simmer, stirring lightly. After 3 minutes, add the noodles directly into the pan and bring to the boil. Cook according to the timings on the packet.

Divide the noodle and sauce mixture between 2 bowls, and top with the bacon and sautéed spinach. Add a raw egg yolk on each and scatter over the grated cheese. Season with pepper and drizzle with olive oil.

Overleaf: Jaja Ramen (left) and Carbonara Ramen (right).

COSY WINTER DRY RAMEN

Serves 2

'Dry ramen' is a term given to dipping noodles, as the ramen noodles are served without sauce 'dry' in a separate dish. This warming recipe is less soupy than some of the ramen bowls but has a flavoursome sauce that envelops the noodles as you dip them.

6 slices pork belly (shop-bought)
1 teaspoon cooking saké
½ medium white onion
1 whole aubergine (eggplant)
2.5 cm (1 in) fresh ginger root
1½ teaspoons vegetable oil
1½ teaspoons sesame oil
210 ml (7½ fl oz/scant 1 cup) water
70 ml (2½ fl oz/scant ⅓ cup) *mentsuyu* (Chinese soup stock), triple concentrate
1 teaspoon kelp (kombu) stock powder
300 g (10½ oz/2 nests) frozen fresh ramen noodles

TOPPINGS

2 teaspoons white sesame seeds
Shichimi togarashi or *yuzu shichimi*

Cut the pork belly into bite-sized pieces, and sprinkle with a little saké. Slice the onion and cube the aubergine. Peel and grate the ginger root.

Place the vegetable and sesame oils in a saucepan over a medium-high heat. Add the pork belly and stir-fry for 1 minute, then add the onion and finally the aubergine for 7–10 minutes until soft.

Add the water, *mentsuyu*, ginger and kelp powder. Reduce the heat and simmer the mixture for 5 minutes over a low heat.

When the pork is cooked through and the aubergine and onion are soft, transfer to 2 serving bowls. Scatter over some white sesame seeds and add a dash of *shichimi togarashi* or *yuzu shichimi*.

Now cook the ramen according to the instructions on the packet and rinse with cold water. Drain and divide between 2 separate plates.

To eat, dip the drained noodles into the soup mix.

CHILLED RAMEN

Serves 2

Chilled ramen is the perfect summer-time dish.
Try this refreshing noodle bowl as an alternative
to a more conventional salad.

½ teaspoon salt
2 teaspoons Japanese soy sauce
4 teaspoons chicken stock powder
800 ml (28 fl oz/3⅓ cups) water
1 teaspoon sesame oil
240 g (8½ oz/2 nests) fresh Chinese
    noodles

TOPPINGS
4 slices roasted pork (shop-bought)
20 g (¾ oz/2 tablespoons) tinned
    bamboo shoots
4 cherry tomatoes, halved
2 Soy-marinated Eggs (*see page 37*)
Chinese chives, chopped

Put the salt, soy sauce, chicken stock powder, water and sesame oil into a pot and heat over a medium heat until nearly boiling. Remove from the heat, allow to cool and then chill in the refrigerator for 15–20 minutes.

Cook the noodles in boiling water according to the instructions on the packet, then drain and rinse thoroughly with cold water. Chill them by immersing in a bowl of iced water.

Divide the chilled noodles in 2 serving bowls and pour over the chilled dashi broth. Top with the slices of pork, bamboo shoots, cherry tomatoes, halved eggs and chopped Chinese chives.

Sometimes referred to as *hiyashi-chuka*, chilled noodles are traditionally served with a vinegary dressing that includes soy sauce and mustard for extra flavour. Slices of ham, cucumber and tomatoes sometimes accompany the noodles to build it out.

WARM BEEF RAMEN

Serves 2

One of the biggest draws of ramen is the concept of a whole
meal in a bowl. This recipe is the perfect example with its
balance of tender beef, vegetables and noodles.

~~~~~~

5 g (¼ oz) dried wood ear mushrooms
250 g (9 oz) beef shin (shank)
Sea salt and ground black pepper
4 bulbs pak choi (bok choy)
2 tablespoons sesame oil plus
    ½ teaspoon
1 tablespoon cornflour (cornstarch)
1 litre (35 fl oz/4¼ cups) water
2 teaspoons chicken stock powder
2 tablespoons cooking saké
4 teaspoons Japanese soy sauce
460 g (16¼ oz) frozen precooked
    udon noodles

TOPPING
Karashi takana (pickled mustard leaves)

Soak the wood ear mushrooms in enough water to just cover them for
about 20 minutes. When they have softened, squeeze the water out,
remove the stalks (stems) and cut the remainder into pieces. Cut the
beef into 5 cm (2 in) wide strips and rub with salt and pepper.

Trim the base off the pak choi and then break it into leaves and stalks.

Now heat 2 tablespoons of the sesame oil in a wok and, when hot, add
the beef strips. Stir-fry over a high heat for 3–5 minutes until golden
brown, then add the pak choi stalks and mushrooms and stir-fry for
about 2 minutes more. Stir-fry quickly and then scatter the cornflour
over the ingredients and stir to coat.

Add the water, chicken stock powder, saké, soy sauce and the remaining
sesame oil, stirring constantly to thicken the beef mixture into a sauce.
Bring it to the boil, then lower the heat.

Cook the noodles according to the instructions on the packet. Drain and
divide between 2 bowls. Pour the warm beef soup over and top with the
karashi takana.

PHO-STYLE BEEF RAMEN

Serves 2

Beef isn't commonly used in ramen dishes but often features
in Vietnamese pho. This slow-cooked fusion dish makes the
perfect recipe for a relaxed weekend cooking session.

1 kg (2¼ lb) beef tendon
50 ml (1¾ fl oz/scant ¼ cup) *mentsuyu*
(Chinese soup stock)
1 litre (35 fl oz/4¼ cups) cold water
300 ml (10 fl oz /1¼ cups) hot water
1 teaspoon chicken stock powder
¼ teaspoon ginger purée
200 g (7 oz) beef strips, or steak cut
into thin strips
240 g (8½ oz/2 nests) Chinese glass
noodles

TOPPINGS
Spring onions (scallions), sliced
Lime wedges
Thai basil sprigs

Make the broth. Place the beef tendon, *mentsuyu* and cold water in
a lidded pot, bring to the boil and simmer, uncovered, for 4 hours.
Alternatively, place in a pressure cooker for 1 hour. Add more water
to the broth if it reduces too much.

Drain the stock through a fine sieve. Discard the beef tendon (all the
meat will absorb into the stock). Now ladle about 300 ml (10 fl oz/1¼cups)
of the broth and the hot water into a pot over a medium-high heat. Add
the chicken stock powder, ginger purée and beef strips, then stir. Bring
back to the boil, stirring occasionally, until the beef is cooked.

Cook the noodles according to the instructions on the packet. Divide
the between 2 serving bowls and pour over the soup. Top with the spring
onions and Thai basil, and serve with lime wedges.

Because of its collagen-rich fibres, beef tendon breaks
down into gelatine when slow-cooked over several
hours, as here. This will give your broth a denser, more
gelatinous feel and create a richer dish.

TAIWAN BEEF NOODLES

Serves 2

A fragrant balance of comfort and freshness, this dish has
its roots in China and became a favourite in Taiwan when
refugees from the Chinese Civil War (1927–1949) missed
the taste of their home-cooked beef noodles.

5 spring onions (scallions)
1 medium white onion
1 large tomato
400 g (14 oz) beef shin (shank), or
    beef round
2.5 cm (1 in) fresh ginger root, unpeeled
1 clove garlic
1 tablespoon vegetable oil
½–1 tablespoon *doubanjiang* (chilli
    bean paste)
500 ml (18 fl oz/2 cups) water
2 tablespoons Japanese soy sauce
1 tablespoon cooking saké
Zest of 1 fresh mandarin orange
1 teaspoon Sichuan peppercorns
1 pak choi (bok choy) bulb, quartered
    lengthways
240 g (8½ oz) udon noodles

TOPPING
Mandarin orange zest

Trim the roots off the spring onions and tie the bunch together with
kitchen twine. Halve the white onion and tomato. Cube the beef shin
(shank) into 3 cm (1¼ in) pieces. Thinly slice the ginger and garlic.

Heat the vegetable oil in a frying pan over a medium-high heat, add the
cubed beef and brown for 1–2 minutes. Add the *doubanjiang* and stir-fry
until combined.

When the mixture is fragrant, tip the contents into a pot, add the water,
soy sauce, saké, onion, tomato and the spring onion bunch.

Using a square of muslin (cheesecloth), make a small spice bag, filling
it with the ginger, garlic, mandarin zest and Sichuan peppercorns. Tie
it with twine and drop it into the broth. Turn the heat to medium and
bring the mixture to the boil.

Once boiling, reduce the temperature to low, cover and simmer for about
1½ hours until the beef is tender. Remove the spice bag, spring onion
bunch and tomato skins, and discard.

Boil plenty of water in another pot and cook the pak choi and the
noodles in the same water according to the timing instructions on the
noodle packet, then drain. Divide the noodles and bok choy into bowls,
spoon over the beef soup and top with orange zest.

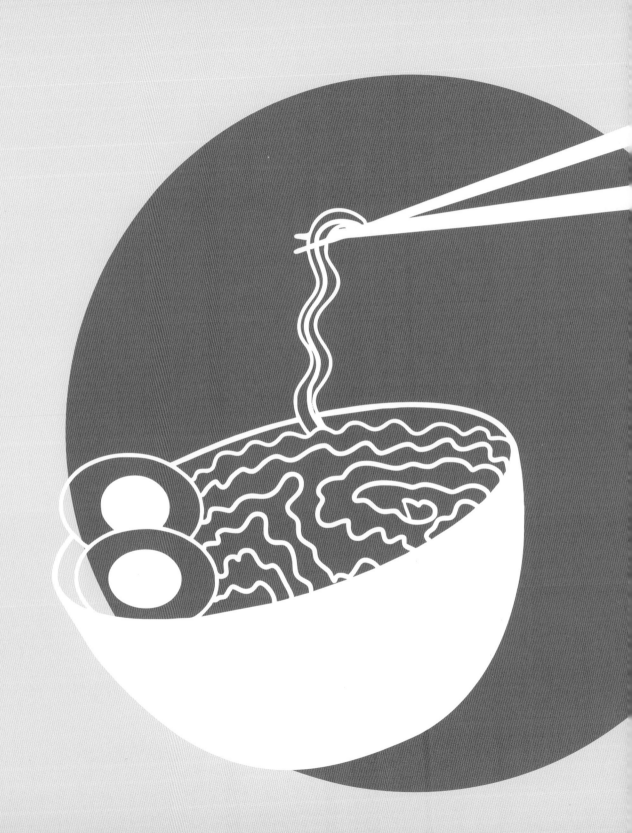

4
SEAFOOD & FISH RAMEN

As with many Asian countries, Japan is an island country, and therefore seafood and fish make up a large part of everyday cuisine. Coupled with the intense flavours of seaweed and the saltiness of soy and dried kelp seasonings, it is no surprise that the fruits of the sea are used to stunning effect in many ramen bowls. This chapter will allow you to experiment with new taste combinations to create beautiful and delicious noodle dishes.

CRAB RAMEN

Serves 2

Crab is a delicacy in Japan. Snow crabs found in the deep, sea waters off the coast of Shimane are only allowed to be fished for four months of the year to sustain stocks. For this recipe, you can use any type of crab, either fresh from a fishmonger or frozen crabmeat from the supermarket.

100 g (3½ oz) king crabmeat
3 broken king crab shell pieces
3 tablespoons cooking saké
800 ml (28 fl oz/3⅓ cups) water
1 tablespoon kelp (kombu) stock powder
100 g (3½ oz/1 cup) bean sprouts
2 spring onions (scallions)
400 g (14 oz) frozen precooked
    udon noodles
1 tablespoon butter
4 tablespoons white miso paste

TOPPINGS
2 Soy-marinated Eggs (*see page 37*)
6–8 slices *narutomaki* (fishcake)
Fresh coriander (cilantro) leaves

If you aren't used to handling crab, ask your fishmonger to dress the crab for you; this way, you will have shredded meat and the shell to use in the stock. The meat in the large front claws is the best. To prepare crab claws, break at the joint, peel off the shell on one side using kitchen scissors and loosen the meat with a crab spoon. (Crab contains gills, often called 'dead man's finger,' which should not be eaten.)

Place a cupful of crab shell pieces and the saké in a pot over a medium-high heat, then add the water and kelp powder and bring to the boil. Reduce the heat and simmer for 30 minutes. Top up with hot water as needed. Turn off the heat and allow to cool for at least 1 hour. Strain and reserve.

Soak the bean sprouts in water for 3 minutes, then drain. Chop the spring onions into small pieces.

Boil plenty of water in a saucepan and cook the noodles according to the instructions on the packet. While they are cooking, melt the butter in another saucepan and quickly fry the bean sprouts and spring onions. Add the strained crab broth and meat. Bring to the boil, then turn off the heat.

Place the miso in a warmed bowl and dissolve with a little of the broth. Pour into the crab broth and mix. Drain the noodles, divide between 2 bowls, then pour over the crab broth. To finish, top each bowl with a halved egg, 3–4 slices of *narutomaki* and coriander leaves.

CRAB & EGG RAMEN

Serves 2

Crab is showcased in multiple ways in Japanese dishes:
fried with rice, as tempura, boiled, steamed and (as here)
in soup broths. This delicate ramen bowl is an delicious
way to enjoy the subtle sweet flavour.

2 medium (US large) eggs
150 ml (5 fl oz/⅔ cup) water
1 tablespoon Japanese soy sauce
1 tablespoon sugar
1½ teaspoons cornflour (cornstarch)
1 teaspoon oyster sauce
½ teaspoon chicken stock powder
300 g (8½ oz/2 nests) frozen
    fresh ramen

TOPPINGS
6 crab sticks (broken up and shredded
    by hand)
1½ teaspoons sesame oil
1 teaspoon rice vinegar

In a bowl, beat the eggs lightly. Then, place the water, soy sauce, sugar, cornflour, oyster sauce, and chicken stock powder in a cold frying pan. Stir them together and then turn on the heat to medium-high, still stirring, until it thickens and comes to the boil. Once thickened, add in the beaten egg little by little. Mix lightly until the egg is almost cooked, then remove from the heat.

Prepare your noodles according to the instructions on the packet, then drain and place in 2 serving bowls.

Layer the egg mixture over the noodles and add the shredded crab sticks. Drizzle over the sesame oil and add drops of rice vinegar.

Crab sticks, called *kanikama* in Japan, are made from finely pulverized white fish (*surimi*) that has been shaped to resemble snow crab legs. Invented in Japan in the 1970s, they are used in salads, soups and sushi.

SALTY SCALLOP RAMEN

Serves 2

Conpoy, or dried scallop, is a popular ingredient in Cantonese cooking and considered a gourmet delicacy, but it is less commonly known in the West. Once you have discovered the delicious seashore aromas in this easy-to-store dried version, you will be converted.

10 *conpoy* (dried scallops), weighing about 50 g (1¾ oz)
800 ml (28 fl oz/3⅓ cups) hot water
2 teaspoons chicken stock powder
2 tablespoons cooking saké
4 teaspoons soy sauce
½ teaspoon sesame oil
1 teaspoon salt
240 g (8½ oz/2 nests) fresh Chinese noodles

TOPPINGS
1 medium (US large) soft-boiled egg
1–2 spring onions (scallions), cut into thin strips

Place the dried scallops in a large heat-resistant bowl with a little cold water to cover and soak for 15 minutes. Cover with cling film (plastic wrap) and heat in a 800W microwave for 2 minutes.

In a separate pan, add the hot water, chicken stock powder, saké, soy sauce, sesame oil and salt. Bring it the boil, then lower the heat. Add the reconstituted scallops over a medium heat. Break them up a little with a spoon and simmer for about 5 minutes. Remove from the heat.

Cook the noodles according to the instructions on the packet. Drain well. Divide the cooked noodles into 2 serving bowls, pour the scallop broth over and top each with half a boiled egg and the spring onions.

Conpoy (dried scallops) are used in sauces and broths for their distinctive flavour (*see also Shio Tare on page 29*). The drying process intensifies the taste and gives them a much deeper, umami flavour and supple, springy texture, compared to the subtle, sweet, softness of the fresh variety we know in the West.

PRAWN RAMEN

Serves 2

Prawns (shrimp), called *ebi*, are a great delicacy and firm favourite in
Japanese cuisine. With many species available, red prawns feature in this
recipe, but you can substitute with other varieties. Leaving the head on
while cooking prawns imparts extra seafood flavour to your dish.

2½ teaspoons Thai red curry paste
1 teaspoon Thai chilli powder
⅛ teaspoon ground black pepper
1 teaspoon garlic powder
½ teaspoon ground ginger
½ teaspoon ground coriander
1 teaspoon powdered coconut milk
6 shell-on red prawn (shrimp) tails,
   weighing about 30 g (1 oz) each
1 tablespoon olive oil
800 ml (28 fl oz/3⅓ cups) water
1 vegetable stock (bouillon) cube
½ teaspoon granulated sugar
1 teaspoon *nam pla* (Thai fish sauce)
1 teaspoon lemon pepper seasoning
300 g (10½ oz) frozen fresh ramen
   noodles

TOPPINGS
Fresh coriander (cilantro) leaves
Shichimi togarashi

Mix the red curry paste, chilli powder, black pepper, garlic powder,
ground ginger, ground coriander and powdered coconut milk in a
mixing bowl, stirring until combined.

If desired, prepare the red prawns by removing the heads and
shells before cooking and reserve these for making into soup stock.
Otherwise use whole praws. Use a cocktail stick (toothpick) to devein
and remove the waste tract.

Heat the olive oil in a deep frying pan, add the prawns and fry for
5 minutes. Once the prawns are cooked and fragrant, transfer them
to a plate.

Add the water, stock cube and the red curry paste mixture to the frying
pan with the oil from the prawns and stir to dissolve over a low heat.
Adjust the taste to your preference with fish sauce and lemon pepper
seasoning, Return the red prawns to the pan and bring to a boil.

Prepare your noodles according to the instructions on the packet, then
divide them between 2 serving bowls. Gently pour over the soup and
prawns. Top with the coriander leaves and scatter with the *shichimi*.

KING PRAWN MISO RAMEN

Serves 2

Succulent king prawns (jumbo shrimp), accompanied by the miso aromas of this dashi, make a mouthwatering treat. A hint of the warming liquor of saké complements the delicate prawn flavour and will enhance any other seafood dishes, too.

8 raw king (tiger) prawns (jumbo shrimp) with heads, weighing about 35 g (1¼ oz) each
30 g (1 oz/2 tablespoons) salted butter
600 ml (20 fl oz/2½ cups) hot water
2 tablespoons saké
2 tablespoons white miso paste
2 teaspoons Japanese soy sauce
2 teaspoons white granulated sugar
½ teaspoon chicken stock powder
240 g (8½ oz/2 nests) fresh Chinese noodles

TOPPINGS
2 spring onions (scallions), sliced
6–8 slices *narutomaki* (fishcake)
Kaiware radish sprouts, cress or microgreens

Remove the head and shell from the prawns. Pull out the black digestive tract from the prawns' spines to devein (*see page 110*).

Put the salted butter in a saucepan over a medium heat, add the prawns and cook until the colour of the prawns changes from grey to pink. Then add the hot water and simmer for about 2 minutes. Remove the prawns and set aside. Strain the liquid and heat over a medium heat. Bring to the boil, stir in the saké, miso, soy sauce, sugar and chicken stock, then add the fried prawns. Remove the pan from the heat when the stock is reduced by about half.

Meanwhile, cook the Chinese noodles according to the instructions on the packet. Drain and divide into 2 serving bowls and spoon over the prawn broth. Top with spring onions, *narutomaki* and radish sprouts.

Large shrimp, like the king prawns used in this recipe, are from the warm waters of Asia, Latin America and the Gulf Coast of the United States.

TUNA TATAKI RAMEN

Serves 2

Japan is a country with a string of islands making up its whole, and this is, naturally enough, the reason fish is so important in the cuisine. Of all fish, tuna is held in the highest esteem. *Tataki* is a method of searing the outside of tuna while leaving the inside a vibrant pink.

2 tablespoons groundnut (peanut) oil or grapeseed oil
150 g (5½ oz) sashimi-grade tuna (ideally cut into a rectangular block)
1 clove garlic
1 medium carrot
1 white onion
1 tablespoon ginger purée
800 ml (28 fl oz/3⅓ cups) water
2 tablespoons soy sauce
1 tablespoon chicken stock powder
1 teaspoon oyster sauce
Pinch of sea salt
Pinch of ground black pepper
2 x 120 g (4¼ oz/2 nests) fresh Chinese noodles

TOPPINGS
Toasted sesame seeds
Fresh coriander (cilantro) leaves
Spring onions (scallions), sliced (optional)

Warm a non-stick frying pan over a medium-high heat and add the groundnut or grapeseed oil. When the oil is hot, sear the block of tuna for 30 seconds on each side. Set the tuna, still in the warm pan, aside for 5 minutes. After the 5 minutes, place the tuna on a plate and refrigerate for a minimum of 20 minutes (this makes it much easier to slice thinly, to display in your ramen bowl).

Transfer the excess oil from the tuna pan into a large saucepan.

Very finely chop the garlic, julienne the carrot and thinly slice the onion. Add to the saucepan with the ginger purée and stir-fry for 5 minutes.

Now add the water, soy sauce, chicken stock powder, oyster sauce and salt and pepper to the pan. Stir for another 5–7 minutes until the carrots soften.

Cook the fresh Chinese noodles according to the instructions on the packet. Drain and divide between 2 serving bowls. Pour the vegetable soup broth over.

Take the tuna out of the fridge and neatly slice into 5 mm (¼ in) slices with a sharp knife. Arrange the tuna over the bowls and top with sesame seeds, coriander and, if desired, chopped spring onions.

CHIGE RAMEN

Serves 2

Chige is often eaten in winter in Japan, much like its Korean counterpart *jjigae*, a stew served boiling hot in a communal dish. It has all the comfort of a hot pot but none of the long wait time. The classic Asian ingredients you will need – canned clams and *gochujang* – are now widely available in supermarkets and worth seeking out, as they add authentic flavours to the dish.

4 spring onions (scallions)
160 g (5½ oz) firm tofu
Cornflour (cornstarch), to dust
500 ml (18 fl oz/2 cups) vegetable oil
2 teaspoons sesame oil
1 teaspoon grated garlic
½ teaspoon grated fresh ginger root
1 teaspoon chilli flakes
1 teaspoon *gochujang* (Korean red
　　chilli paste)
1 x 110 g (4 oz) jar whole baby clams
800 ml (28 fl oz/3⅓ cups) water
2 teaspoons chicken stock powder
240 g (8½ oz/2 nests) fresh Chinese
　　noodles
120 g (4 oz) roasted pork belly slices
　　(shop-bought)

TOPPINGS

1 tablespoon sesame seeds
Chinese chives, snipped
Dried chilli flakes and sliced fresh
　　red chillies

Cut the spring onions into short 2 cm (¾ in) lengths. Cut the tofu into bite-sized cubes. Sandwich the tofu between dry kitchen paper towels and press to remove as much moisture as possible; repeat. Roll the tofu in cornflour to dust. Heat the oil to about 170°C (340°F) or until a little cornflour sizzles in the oil. Once hot, add the tofu cubes and fry for 2–3 minutes until golden. Drain on a wire rack or kitchen paper towels.

In a bowl, combine the sesame oil, garlic, ginger, chilli flakes, *gochujang* and clams (with their juice).

Boil the water, add the chicken stock and noodles, and bring back to the boil. After 1 minute, place the pork belly slices, spring onions and crab mixture into the pot, and simmer for 2 minutes more. Divide between 2 serving bowls. Top with the tofu, sesame seeds, chives and chilli.

Ready-made, deep-fried tofu can be found in Asian markets. The precooked cubes can be reheated in a broth or stir-fried a few minutes before serving.

SEAFOOD RAMEN

Serves 2

Authentic Japanese fish broths often include golden snapper and shellfish, such as clams, but any seafood mix, such as salmon, white fish and crustaceans, will work well. You can make this tasty, saké-infused dish as and when you like. It is perfect for when you need to whizz up a midweek supper.

400 g (14 oz) frozen seafood mix of fish, mussels, squid and prawns (shrimp)
2 tablespoons saké or white wine
1 medium white onion
2 tablespoons vegetable oil
2 tablespoons grated fresh ginger root
2 tablespoons grated garlic
1 litre (35 fl oz/4¼ cups) water
1 teaspoon Japanese soy sauce
2 teaspoons bonito stock powder
2 teaspoons vegetable stock powder or 1 vegetable stock (bouillon) cube
400 g (14 oz) frozen precooked udon noodles or 240 g (8½ oz/2 nests) Chinese fresh noodles

TOPPINGS

6–8 slices *kamaboko* (fishcake)
2 Spice-seasoned Eggs (*see page 37*)
Pinch of ground black pepper
Spring onions (scallions), sliced
1 tablespoon *tobiko* (fish roe)

Defrost the seafood mix and then soak in the saké for 30 minutes.

Cut the onion into wedges and fry in a saucepan with the vegetable oil. When softened, add the ginger and garlic. Strain the seafood and add it to the saucepan, reserving the liquid. Fry for 3–4 minutes more.

Now add the water, soy sauce, bonito stock powder, vegetable stock powder, and the reserved seafood saké liquid. Simmer until everything is fragrant and completely heated through.

Prepare the noodles according to the instructions on the packet. Once cooked, drain well and divide between 2 serving bowls.

Spoon the seafood soup over the noodles. Arrange the *kamaboko* and halved boiled eggs on top, add pepper and scatter over the chopped spring onions. Serve with the fish roe.

Overleaf: Chige Ramen (left) and Seafood Ramen (right).

GINGER FISH RAMEN

Serves 2

Sea bream, called *tai*, is a traditional Japanese seafood ingredient, used in celebrations to usher in good luck. Its vibrant red hues and elegant shape lend it its special status. Here the delicate sea flavours are enhanced with a broth made with dried kelp leaves and wafer-thin bonito flakes.

1 whole sea bream or sea bass on the bone but without the head, weighing 700 g (1½ lb)

1 teaspoon salt, for coating the fish, plus extra 1¼ teaspoons for seasoning

1 litre (35 fl oz/4¼ cups) water

8 g (¼ oz) dried kelp leaf (kombu)

5 g (¼ oz/⅓cup) bonito flakes (*katsuobushi*)

Sea salt

1 teaspoon cooking saké

240 g (8½ oz/2 nests) fresh Chinese noodles

TOPPINGS

1 spring onion (scallion), sliced

6–8 slices fresh ginger root

Pickled ginger (optional)

Sprinkle the sea bream with 1 teaspoon of salt and refrigerate for 30 minutes.

Soak the whole fish in a shallow bowl of hot water (about 90°C/195°F) for 7–10 minutes, then remove from the water and rub away any sliminess.

Fill a pot with the water, add the dried kelp and fish and cook over a low heat for about 10 minutes. Bring to the boil, remove the kelp and scoop off any scum. Reduce the heat to low and cook for another 10 minutes, then add the bonito flakes and bring back to the boil.

Once boiling, remove the dried bonito flakes, which will be floating on the surface. Turn off the heat and season the liquid with the 1¼ teaspoons of salt and the saké. Leave for 5 minutes, then lift out the fish and gently fork the flesh from the bones. Strain the liquid to create the broth.

Meanwhile, boil the noodles in another pot according to the instructions on the packet. When the noodles are cooked, drain and divide them between 2 serving bowls. Pour the soup stock over and add the flaked fish on top of the noodles. Finish with spring onion, thinly sliced ginger and, if desired, pickled ginger.

SALMON & PAK CHOI RAMEN

Serves 2

The gorgeously fresh and light flavours of saké-infused salmon, ginger and pak choi make this the ultimate refined and delicate ramen bowl. In the West, we associate salmon with Japanese sushi, but this wasn't always the case. Until 1995, when the Norwegian fishing industry promoted it as a raw sushi ingredient to the Japanese food industry, it had only been eaten cooked in Japan.

2 skinless salmon fillets, weighing 260 g (9 oz)
1 tablespoon cooking saké
Pinch of salt, plus 1 teaspoon
2 bulbs pak choi (bok choy)
4 spring onions (scallions)
5 cm (2 in) fresh ginger root
2 tablespoons sesame oil
350 ml (fl oz/1½ cups) water
2 teaspoons chicken stock powder or 1 chicken stock (bouillon) cube
500 ml (18 fl oz/2 cups) soya milk
240 g (8½ oz/2 nests) fresh Chinese noodles

TOPPINGS
White sesame seeds
Kaiware radish sprouts, cress or microgreens
Grated fresh ginger root

Cut each salmon fillet into 4–5 pieces and sprinkle with 1 tablespoon of saké and a pinch of salt. Rub lightly with your hands and leave for about 10 minutes. Next, wipe off any juice from the fish with kitchen paper towel.

Break the pak choi into stalks (stems) and leaves, and cut the stalks into 6 equal parts lengthways. Slice the spring onions diagonally into 1 cm (½ in) strips. Peel the ginger and cut into thin slices.

Heat the sesame oil in a frying pan over a medium heat, add the ginger, salmon, pak choi and spring onions in that order and stir-fry for 5–7 minutes in total until the fish is evenly cooked. Pour in the water, chicken stock powder and the 1 teaspoon of salt. Bring to the boil and add the soya milk, mixing quickly. Turn the heat down and simmer.

Meanwhile cook the noodles according to the instructions on the packet. Strain and divide between 2 serving bowls.

Add the salmon and pak choi broth over the top. Finish with white sesame seeds, radish sprouts and grated ginger.

SQUID & KALE RAMEN

Serves 2

Squid, or *surume ika*, is one of Japan's most popular seafoods. Tenderized in a milk bath and simmered gently, this recipe guarantees soft and tender squid for the perfect ramen bowl.

500 g (18 oz) squid (cleaned)

400 ml (14 fl oz/1⅔ cups) full-fat (whole) milk

1 white onion

1 clove garlic

5 cm (2 in) fresh ginger root

150 g (5½ oz) curly kale

2 fresh red bird's-eye chillies

2 tablespoons sesame oil

800 ml (28 fl oz/3⅓ cups) water

2 tablespoons sesame oil

2 teaspoon chicken stock powder

2 teaspoons bonito stock powder

2 x 120 g (4¼ oz/2 nests) fresh Chinese noodles

TOPPINGS

1 teaspoon bonito flakes (*katsuobushi*)

Spring onions (scallions), sliced

Sliced red bird's-eye chillies

Make sure the squid is clean by rinsing it well under cold, running water and then cut it into 1 cm (1½ in) thick rings. You can cut the tentacle sections in half as well, if they are little long.

Pour the milk into a bowl and soak the squid into it for a minimum of 30 minutes. This will ensure the squid is tender soft once cooked. Remove the squid from the milk and pat dry with a kitchen paper towel.

Thinly slice the white onion, garlic and ginger. Chop the kale into bite-sized pieces. Deseed and thinly slice the red chillies diagonally.

Heat 1 tablespoon of the sesame oil in a deep, heavy-based frying pan over a medium heat and add the onion to the pan. Stir with a wooden spoon for 3–4 minutes or until the onion is translucent. Now add the sliced garlic, ginger and chillies and stir for another 1 minute or so.

Pour the water into the frying pan and spoon in the remaining sesame oil. Add the chicken and bonito stock powders. Simmer for 5 minutes. Add the kale and the sliced squid. Simmer for another 5–7 minutes.

Meanwhile cook the ramen noodles according to the instructions on the packet. Drain and divide between 2 serving bowls. Pour the squid and kale soup over the noodles and top with the bonito flakes, spring onions and chilli. (The bonito flakes will move, fluttering and 'dancing' from contact with the heat.)

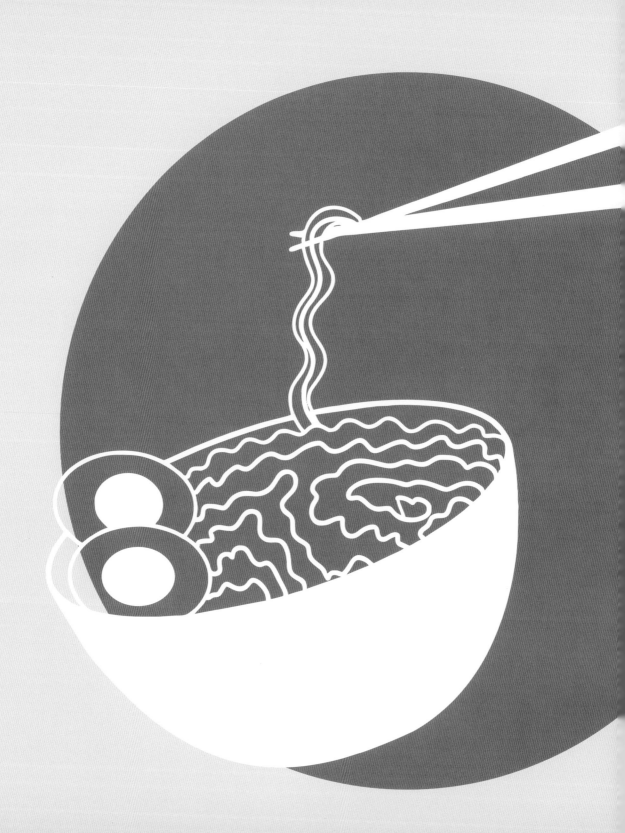

5
VEGAN &
VEGETARIAN
RAMEN

Vegetarian and vegan cooking has a long tradition
in Asia, and there are plenty of vegetables to enjoy
in a bowl of ramen, from the refreshing, light
crunch of pak choi (bok choy) or the salty umami
depth of nori and kelp, to the extraordinary beauty
and earthiness of shimeji and shiitake mushrooms.
The recipes in this chapter will help you to indulge
and showcase a love of meat-free cooking.

VEGETABLE GARDEN RAMEN

Serves 2

This vegan dish showcases the colour and texture of garden and sea vegetables with the added umami depth of seaweed, miso and soy. Crispy dried onions are a great storecupboard ingredient and add a final, tangy, crunchy topping.

2 cloves garlic
½ white onion
1 medium carrot
4 stalks (stems) long-stem broccoli
2 tablespoons sesame oil
2 tablespoons ground sesame seeds
1 litre (35 fl oz/4¼ cups) water
1 x 10 cm (4 in) sheet dried kelp sheet
4 whole dried shiitake mushrooms, rehydrated in lukewarm water for 20 minutes
240 g (8½ oz/2 nests) fresh Chinese noodles
235 ml (8 fl oz/1 cup) soya milk
2 tablespoons white miso paste
4 teaspoons Japanese soy sauce

TOPPINGS
Handful bean sprouts, washed
2 spring onions (scallions), finely sliced
6 bamboo shoots
½ teaspoon white pepper
2 tablespoons dried crispy onions
I teaspoon Chilli Oil (*see page 30*)

Grate the garlic. Slice the onion thinly, julienne the carrot and trim the broccoli slightly so the stems fit in a bowl.

Heat the sesame oil in a frying pan and add the garlic, onion, carrot and broccoli. Fry over a low heat for 10–15 minutes until they soften. Scatter the ground sesame seeds over the vegetables in the pan and fry for another 3 minutes.

Put the water, whole kelp sheet and dried shiitake mushrooms in a pot and simmer over a low heat for 10 minutes.

In the meantime, cook the noodles according to the instructions on the packet. Drain and divide between 2 serving bowls.

Add the soya milk, miso and soy sauce to the broth and bring back to the boil again. Turn off the heat.

Pour the soup over the noodles, then top with bean sprouts, spring onions and bamboo shoots. Season with white pepper, add a small mound of dried crispy onions and drizzle over a few drops of chilli oil.

SILKEN TOFU RAMEN

Serves 2

The art of tofu-making first appeared in Japan in the Nara period (710–794 CE) but silken tofu was created much later, in the 1950s. The cold sauce of this ramen dish is beautifully nutty-tasting, rich and nurturing and creates a silky-smooth soup to spoon over a bowl of noodles.

~~~~~~

1 x 340 g (12 oz) block silken tofu
100 ml (3 ⅓ fl oz/scant ½ cup) full-fat (whole) milk
1 teaspoon tahini or Japanese sesame paste (*neri goma*)
1 teaspoon smooth peanut butter
1 teaspoon sugar
Pinch of salt
240 g (8½ oz/2 nests) fresh Chinese noodles

TOPPINGS

1 medium hard-boiled egg
1 cucumber, julienned
2 teaspoons toasted sesame seeds
Sesame oil

Add the tofu, milk, sesame paste, peanut butter, sugar, salt and 2 ice cubes to a blender. Blitz to a smooth consistency. It should still be slightly thick for this recipe, but you can add more milk if you prefer a runnier soup base.

Cook the noodles according to the instructions on the packet. Drain and run them under cold water.

Divide the noodles between 2 serving bowls and add the tofu mixture. Top each bowl with half a boiled egg, cucumber strips, sesame seeds and a drizzle of sesame oil.

~~~~~~

Tofu blocks are made in a process similar to cheese-making but use the non-dairy ingredient of curdled soya milk. A staple Japanese ingredient, tofu is especially important in Japan's Buddhist temple cuisine (known as *shojin ryori*), where the concept of nonviolence disapproves of the use of animals as food.

COLD TAN TAN NOODLES

Serves 2

Packing a serious flavour punch with very little effort, this vegan
version of *tan tan* is based on Sichuan spicy *dan dan* noodles but
without any meat ingredients. The creamy noodles are served
cold with a spicy mushroom topping.

1 tablespoon vegetable oil
1 teaspoon grated fresh ginger root
1 garlic clove, finely chopped
300 g (10½ oz) white mushrooms, such
    as shimeji, rinsed and trimmed
1 tablespoon *doubanjiang* (chilli
    bean paste)
1 tablespoon soy sauce
1 tablespoon cooking saké
140 g (8½ oz) dried Korean thin noodles
2 tablespoons white miso paste
600 ml (20 fl oz/2 ½ cups) soya milk
2 teaspoons vegetarian stock powder
1 tablespoon ground sesame seeds
2 tablespoons white miso powder

TOPPING
1 teaspoon Chilli Oil (*see page 30*)

Heat the oil in a frying pan over a high heat and add the ginger, garlic
and mushrooms, stir-frying for 2–3 minutes. Add the *doubanjiang*, soy
sauce and saké. Reduce the heat to low and continue cooking until all
the liquid has absorbed. Set aside.

Boil the noodles for 3 minutes, then drain and run under cold water. Place
the miso paste, soya milk, stock powder and sesame seeds in a bowl and
mix together with a fork. Divide the noodles between 2 serving bowls
and add the miso-milk mixture along with the miso powder. Toss gently
to combine. Top with the mushrooms and drizzle with the chilli oil.

Dan dan, the Chinese original of Japanese *tan tan*, is
a drier version that is similar to the reduced sauce
and rice cakes made in slow-cookers and sold by the
bag at Korean food stands. Meat spiced with Sichuan
pepper, cinnamon sticks and star anise, *dan dan*
traditionally would be carried by street vendors along
with baskets of noodles to sell.

GET WELL SOON RAMEN

Serves 2

Just as grandmother's chicken soup is a go-to home remedy
for colds and flu, this noodle bowl is a great vegan alternative,
full of nourishing goodness. It is topped with ginger, which has
been shown to help ease the symptoms of a cold.

4 Chinese cabbage leaves
1 large carrot
1 large stalk celery
1 small white onion
1 teaspoon sesame oil for frying,
    plus ½ teaspoon
Sea salt and ground black pepper
1 litre (35 fl oz/4¼ cups) water
2 teaspoons vegan stock powder
2 tablespoons cooking saké
4 teaspoons soy sauce
70 g (2½ oz/2½ cups) fresh spinach
300 g (10½ oz) frozen fresh ramen
    noodles

TOPPINGS
Grated fresh ginger root
Sliced spring onions (scallions), optional

Chop the Chinese cabbage leaves, carrot, celery and onion into 1 cm
(½ in) widths.

Heat 1 teaspoon of sesame oil in a deep frying pan or wok and fry the
vegetables for about 3–4 minutes until they soften slightly but still retain
some crunch. Season the vegetables as they cook with salt and pepper.

When the vegetables are soft, pour in the water and add the vegan stock
powder, saké, soy sauce and the ½ teaspoon of sesame oil, and stir. Bring
to the boil, then add the noodles and spinach and cook for 3 minutes.

Divide the noodles and soup between 2 serving bowls, top with grated
ginger and spring onion slices, if desired, and serve.

A vegetable-based broth delivers a boost of nutrients
such as vitamins and minerals and increases your
liquid intake. It is also a great way to use up any
leftover vegetables you may have.

DIET RAMEN

Serves 2

This recipe provides a wonderful texture and crunch with
shimeji mushrooms and bean sprouts contrasting with
creamy egg and soft noodles. It will fill you up and satisfy your
appetite and taste buds without the addition of processed fats.

75 g (2½ oz) shimeji mushrooms
300 g (10½ oz/3 cups) bean sprouts
2 medium (US large) eggs
1 tablespoon sesame oil
800 ml (28 fl oz/3⅓ cups) water
2 teaspoons vegetable stock powder
2 tablespoons cooking saké
4 teaspoons soy sauce
½ teaspoon sesame oil
240 g (8½ oz/2 nests) fresh Chinese
   noodles

TOPPING
1–2 spring onions (scallions), sliced

Rinse the shimeji mushrooms, trim off the base, then slice into small
pieces. Rinse the bean sprouts. Break the eggs into a bowl and lightly beat.

Heat 1 tablespoon of sesame oil in a frying pan over a medium heat.
When hot, add the bean sprouts and shimeji mushrooms, and stir-fry
for about 1 minute. Season with a little salt, add the beaten egg and mix
well. When the egg is just cooked, turn off the heat.

In the meantime, add the water, vegetable stock powder, saké, soy sauce
and sesame oil to a saucepan and bring to the boil. Simmer for a couple
of minutes and then add the fresh ramen directly into the broth and
cook according to the instructions on the packet.

Once ready, divide between 2 bowls. Top each bowl with the tasty
stir-fried ingredients, and scatter over the spring onions.

Shimeji mushrooms have small round caps and long,
slender stalks (stems) that grow from a connected
base and a nutty flavour and crunchy texture. Their
delicate shapes add beauty to the finished dish.

AUBERGINE MISO RAMEN

Serves 2

Some of the most popular varieties of aubergine (eggplant) in Asian
cuisine include black egg, shoya long and Orient Express, a slender
version that is a deep purple-black. No matter which version you choose,
this dish celebrates the vegetable's distinctive, soft and smoky flavours.

1 whole aubergine (eggplant), weighing
    about 300–400 g (10½–14 oz)
4 teaspoons cornflour (cornstarch)
3 tablespoons vegetable oil
300 g (10½ oz) of frozen fresh ramen
    noodles

GARLIC-SOY SAUCE
50 ml (1¾ fl oz/scant ¼ cup) water
1 tablespoon granulated sugar
2 tablespoons Japanese
    soy sauce
1 tablespoon mirin
½ teaspoon garlic purée

TOPPING
Chinese chives, cut into 4 cm
    (1½ in) strips

Chop the aubergine into bite-sized chunks and soak in a bowl of cold
water for about 5 minutes. In another bowl, make the sauce. Mix
together the water, sugar, soy sauce, mirin and garlic purée. Set aside.

Drain the aubergine and place it in a sealed bag with the cornflour.
Give the bag a good shake to coat the aubergine.

Heat the vegetable oil in a frying pan, add the aubergine and fry for
3–4 minutes, until cooked and golden brown. Drain on a kitchen paper
towel, pressing lightly to get rid of any excess oil.

Prepare your ramen noodles according to the instructions on the packet.
Drain and divide between 2 serving bowls. Pour over the sauce mixture
and top with the aubergine and Chinese chives.

> Japanese aubergine tends to have a thinner skin than
> those in the West. It takes on flavour well, especially
> with dishes like the delicious *nasu dengaku*, where the
> vegetable is glazed with miso and sesame.

PUMPKIN MISO RAMEN

Serves 2

With its spiced pumpkin flavours, this is a perfect dish
for autumnal days. The ultimate in comfort food with the
warmth of ginger and savoury goodness of miso.

~~~~~~

800 g (28 oz) pumpkin
5 cm (2 in) fresh ginger root
500 ml (18 fl oz/2 cups) water
300 g (10½ oz) frozen fresh ramen
    noodles
1½ tablespoons white miso paste
1½ teaspoons kelp (kombu) stock powder

TOPPINGS
1–2 spring onions (scallions), sliced
1–2 teaspoons toasted sesame seeds
Furikake

Peel and deseed the pumpkin and dice the flesh into 2.5 cm (1 in) pieces.
Slice the ginger root thinly. Bring the water to a boil in a saucepan, add
the ginger slices and simmer for 2 minutes.

Add in the diced pumpkin and continue to cook until the pumpkin
softens. Meanwhile, in a separate saucepan, cook the noodles according
to the instructions on the packet. Drain well.

Remove a few cubes of the cooked pumpkin and mash with the miso and
kelp powder in a mixing bowl, then toss in the cooked noodles to coat.

Divide the noodles between 2 serving bowls and pour over the remaining
cooked pumpkin and liquid. Top with sliced spring onions and sesame
seeds. Scatter over the *furikake*.

Roasted pumpkin slices, seasoned with soy sauce,
white miso paste and brown sugar, make a delicious
topping for ramen too. Simply roast them in a hot
oven for about 20 minutes until charred at the edges.

MUSHROOM MISO RAMEN

Serves 2

Me de taberu Nihonjin, or 'We eat with our eyes', is a popular
saying in Japan. This delicate bowl has beautiful stalks (stems),
trumpets and caps of mushrooms floating in an umami broth.

150 g (5 oz) shiitake mushrooms
150 g (5 oz) shimeji mushrooms
150 g (5 oz) oyster mushrooms
2½ tablespoons white miso paste
2 tablespoons cooking saké
1½ tablespoons sugar
1½ teaspoons Japanese soy sauce
½ tablespoon sesame oil, plus 2
    teaspoons for frying
240 g (8½ oz/2 nests) fresh Chinese
    noodles
1 litre (34 fl oz/4 cups) water
4 teaspoons vegetable stock powder
½ teaspoon salt

TOPPING
2 spring onions (scallions), sliced

Cut off the stalks (stems) of the shiitake and shimeji mushrooms and
roughly chop them. Roughly chop the oyster mushrooms. Place the
miso, saké, sugar, soy sauce and sesame oil in a bowl and mix well.

Heat the 2 teaspoons of sesame oil in a frying pan over a medium heat
and add all the mushrooms. Fry for 4–5 minutes until soft.

Add the miso mixture over the mushrooms and stir-fry over a medium
heat for another 3 minutes. When the flavours start to become aromatic
and coat the mushrooms, remove from the heat and set aside.

Cook the noodles according to the instructions on the packet.
Drain and divide between 2 serving bowls.

Fill another saucepan with the water over a medium heat and add
the vegetable powder stock and salt, mixing well. Bring to the boil.

Once boiling, remove from the heat and pour over the noodles.
Pile the miso mushrooms in the middle of each bowl and scatter
the spring onions on top.

FLOATING EGG RAMEN

Serves 2

The egg in this recipe adds a delicious richness to the ramen dish. Soy, powdered kelp and garlic add a deeply umami flavour to counter the mild beaten egg.

~~~~~~

2 cloves garlic
500 ml (18 fl oz/2 cups) water
1 tablespoon mirin
2 tablespoons Japanese soy sauce
1 teaspoon kelp (kombu) stock powder
2 teaspoons cornflour (cornstarch)
2 medium (US large) eggs
300 g (10½ oz) frozen fresh ramen noodles

TOPPING
1 spring onion (scallion), chopped

Grate the garlic. Put the water, mirin, soy sauce, kelp powder and garlic into a saucepan and bring to the boil.

Add a little water to the cornflour in a cup, stir to dissolve into a paste and slowly add it to the saucepan.

Beat the eggs in a bowl and pour them slowly into the saucepan. They will cook almost immediately from the heat of the soup.

Cook the noodles according to the instructions on the packet. Drain and divide between 2 serving bowls. Pour over the floating egg soup and finish with the chopped spring onion.

Floating or dropping egg into soup is a favourite way for Japanese people to add a nourishing, silky texture to a broth or soup. *Kakitamajiru* (Japanese egg-drop soup) combines dashi broth with fluffy beaten egg.

Overleaf: Mushroom Miso Ramen (left) and Floating Egg Ramen (right).

MEAT-FREE CARBONARA

Serves 2

This fusion recipe blends Japanese ramen noodles with flavours of a meat-free Italian carbonara. You can use any vegetarian hard cheese you might have in the fridge and even mozzarella if that is what you have to hand.

240 grams (8½ oz/2 nests) fresh Chinese noodles
600 ml (20 fl oz/2½ cups) water
2 teaspoons vegetable stock powder
2 tablespoons cooking saké
4 teaspoons soy sauce
½ teaspoon sesame oil
2 tablespoons grated vegetarian Cheddar cheese
2 egg yolks
2 tablespoons butter

TOPPINGS
Extra grated vegetarian Cheddar cheese
Freshly ground black pepper

Cook the noodles until they are still slightly al dente and then strain in a colander.

In a saucepan add the water, vegetable stock powder, saké, soy sauce and sesame oil and bring to the boil, stirring well. Now place the warm noodles into 2 serving bowls and pour the broth base over them.

Add 1 egg yolk, 1 tablespoon butter and 1 tablespoon grated cheese to each bowl and mix well. The cheese will start to melt. Finish by scattering over extra grated cheese and a grinding of black pepper.

Most of the cheese in Japan is produced in Tokachi, a region with a similarly cool climate to Europe. Familiar versions of Camembert, Cheddar and parmesan are made, alongside Asian varieties, where the cheese is infused with Japanese dashi.

COLD SHIO RAMEN

Serves 2

If you like the refreshing chilled taste of Spanish gazpacho
or Polish cucumber soup, you will love this noodle recipe.
It's the perfect bowl for a hot day as crushed ice is added
over the finished bowl to cool it to perfection.

600 ml (20 fl oz/2½ cups) water
2 teaspoons vegetable stock powder
2 tablespoons cooking saké
4 teaspoons soy sauce
½ teaspoon sesame oil
450 ml (15 fl oz/2 cups) cold water
240 g (8½ oz) thin Korean
    somen noodles

TOPPINGS
2 medium (US large) soft-boiled eggs
2 spring onions (scallions), sliced
1 tablespoon ground sesame seeds
Sesame oil
Crushed ice

Add the water, vegetable stock powder, saké, soy sauce and sesame oil
to a saucepan and bring to the boil, stirring well. Allow it to simmer for
about 15 minutes to reduce, as this broth is slightly more concentrated
than others. Set aside and allow to cool.

In a separate saucepan, cook the somen noodles according to the
instructions on the packet. Drain and rinse for a couple of minutes
under cold running water. Toss the noodles in the cold soup base,
allowing it to coat well.

Divide the noodles and soup between 2 serving bowls and top each with
an egg, halved. Scatter over the spring onions and sesame seeds. Drizzle
with sesame oil for a hint of flavour, and top with a little crushed ice.

Grinding sesame seeds helps release their beneficial
omega 3 fatty acids, minerals and antioxidants. It also
releases their natural oils, which makes them a useful
thickening agent when added to broths.

MUSHROOM TEMPURA RAMEN

Serves 2

The earthy, nutty taste of mushrooms is always reassuring but this noodle bowl takes them to the next level. The delicate bouquets of slender Japanese and Chinese varieties like enoki, create a visually stunning end result, guaranteed to impress.

300 g (10½ oz) enoki mushroom
100 g (3½ oz) shiitake mushroom
100 g (3½ oz) shimeji mushrooms
300 ml (10½ fl oz/1¼ cups) vegetable oil
150 g (5½ oz/1¼ cups) tempura flour
1 teaspoon garlic powder
200 ml (7 fl oz/scant 1 cup) chilled water
1 clove garlic
2 tablespoon sesame oil
Pinch of sea salt
800 ml (28 fl oz/3⅓ cups) water
3 teaspoons white miso paste
1 tablespoon bonito powder
1 tablespoon tahini
300 g (10½ oz/2 nests) frozen fresh ramen
    noodles

TOPPINGS
2 handfuls fresh coriander (cilantro)
    leaves, chopped
Shichimi togarashi or *furikake*

Rinse the mushrooms to clean, then drain on kitchen paper towel and pat dry. Divide the enoki mushrooms into little clumps.

Heat the oil in a high-sided pan to 170–180°C (340–356°F). Put the tempura flour and garlic powder into a large bowl, mix together and then add the chilled water. Whisk the flour and water until it is silky smooth. Dip the enoki mushrooms into the tempura batter bowl, a few clumps at a time. Shake each clump a little as you take it out of the batter to remove any excess, then drop into the hot oil. Cook each batch until golden, then remove from the oil. Set on kitchen paper towel to drain.

Very finely chop the garlic, thinly slice the shiitake mushrooms and separate out the shimeji mushrooms. Then warm a large frying pan over low–medium heat. Add the sesame oil and garlic and fry for a minute or so before adding the shiitake and shimeji with a pinch of salt. Stir for 3–4 minutes, then set aside.

Place the water, miso, bonito powder and tahini in a large saucepan over a medium-high heat and simmer gently for 3 minutes (do not allow it to come to the boil).

Cook the noodles according to the instructions on the packet. Drain and divide between 2 serving bowls. Pour over the soup, add the fried and tempura mushrooms and scatter over the coriander and *shichimi*.

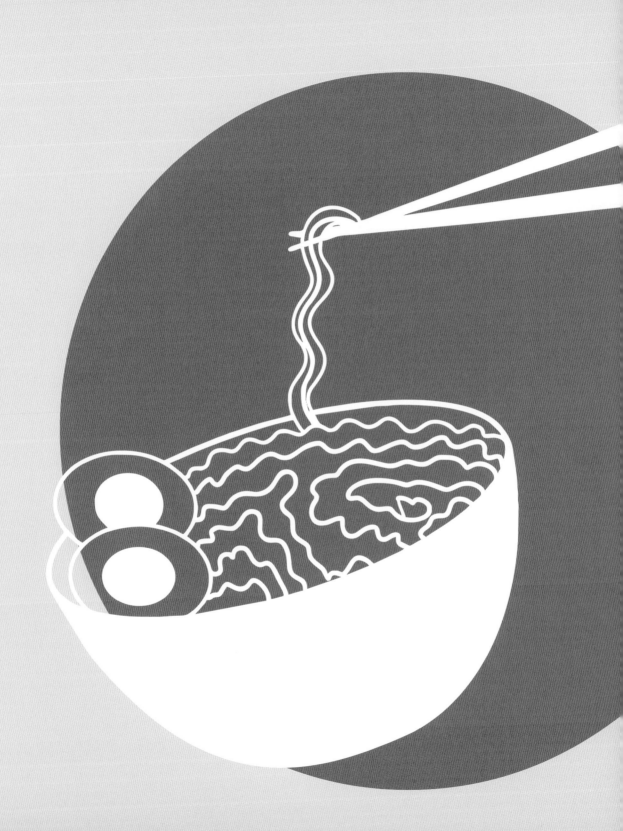

6

INSTANT RAMEN *PLUS*

Who doesn't want the intense flavours and satisfaction of a great ramen bowl in an instant? Taking inspiration from ramen recipes on social media and from pop culture, here are easy ideas and hacks for pimping up shop-bought instant ramen noodle packs. Keep a selection of condiments and toppings to hand and then raid your storecupboard or freezer to create inspiring, tasty, quick noodles any time of the day or night.

MOZZARELLA & TOMATO RAMEN

Serves 2

Oozy melting mozzarella tops this bowl of savoury noodles
and provides a mild contrast to the umami flavours of miso.
It is simple to prepare and baked under the grill (broiler).

2 tomatoes
100 g (3½ oz) firm-block
   mozzarella cheese
600 ml (20 fl oz/2½ cups) water
2 x 140 g (5 oz) instant ramen noodles
   (miso flavour)
2 x instant ramen soup sachets
   (miso flavour)
2 x instant ramen oil seasoning sachets
   (if included)
Extra virgin olive oil, to drizzle

TOPPINGS
Chilli Oil or Aromatic Oil (*see page 30*)
Fresh flat-leaf parsley, finely chopped
Shichimi togarashi

Preheat the oven grill (broiler) to high. Chop the tomatoes and slice the mozzarella cheese.

Boil the water in a saucepan, then add the instant noodles and soup sachets. Transfer the cooked ramen to a deep ovenproof dish. Place the tomatoes and cheese on top, and drizzle over olive oil. Bake under a hot grill until the cheese melts.

Drizzle over the oil seasoning sachet. If your instant ramen doesn't include this seasoning, then add a drizzle of chilli oil or aromatic oil over the noodle bowls.

Top with fresh parsley and *shichimi*.

Shichimi seasoning is a Japanese spice mix that dates back to the seventeenth century and was originally made bespoke for each customer to scatter over soups, noodles and rice dishes. Spicy and flavourful, it usually contains seven spices, with red chilli being the most dominant, but others include orange or yuzu peel, sesame seeds, ground ginger, seaweed and poppy seeds. It can be purchased from most Asian supermarkets.

CHAR SIU PORK RAMEN

Serves 2

This quick-fry pork belly recipe is a speedy way to enjoy that *char siu* flavour in moments. The pork belly is cut into pieces, allowing it to reach that scorched golden colour in minutes. *Char siu* marinade is traditionally used with pork, but it could be used on any type of meat.

80–100 g (3–3½ oz) thinly sliced pork belly
1–2 teaspoons vegetable oil
2 teaspoons grated garlic or garlic purée
1 teaspoon cooking saké or white wine
2 teaspoons granulated sugar
1 teaspoon Japanese soy sauce
Pinch of chicken stock powder
1 teaspoon five-spice powder
2 x 140 g (5 oz) instant ramen noodles
    (soy sauce flavour)
2 x instant ramen soup sachets
    (soy sauce flavour)

TOPPINGS
2 tablespoons wakame seaweed,
    rehydrated for 5 minutes in cold water

Cut the sliced pork belly into bite-sized pieces. Heat the vegetable oil in a frying pan, add the garlic and fry the pork for 5 minutes on both sides, turning once to allow each side to get golden and crisp the edges. Stir in the saké, sugar, soy sauce, chicken stock powder and five-spice powder. Cook for several minutes more and set aside.

Boil the ramen according to the instructions on the packet, drain. In a separate bowl, make up the soup using the soup mix sachets, included in the instant noodle packets, according to the instructions.

Pour the soup into bowls, add the noodles, and top with the *char siu* pork and the wakame.

Chinese five-spice powder was created to hit the five taste zones of sweet, bitter, sour, salty and savoury. It is usually made up of star anise, cloves, Chinese cinnamon, Sichuan pepper and fennel seeds, but there are multiple variations of this core blend.

MISO MILK CURRY RAMEN

Serves 2

Miso and seaweed are at the heart of many Japanese dishes and transport the senses in a moment. Wakame seaweed used in this dish is a species of kelp found in the cooler seas of the Northwest Pacific Ocean. Enjoy it here scattered over this deeply savoury noodle dish.

1 tablespoon Japanese curry powder
2 x instant ramen soup sachets
 (miso flavour)
250 ml (9 fl oz/generous 1 cup) water
500 ml (18 fl oz/2 cups) full-fat (whole)
 milk or soya milk
2 x 140 g (5 oz) instant ramen noodles
 (miso flavour)

TOPPINGS
300 g (10½ oz/3 cups) bean sprouts
6 slices roasted pork (shop-bought)
2 tablespoons wakame seaweed,
 rehydrated for 5 minutes in cold water
1 tablespoon butter

Put the curry powder and miso sachets from the instant ramen packets in a saucepan with the water over a medium heat.

Stir gently until everything has dissolved. Add the milk, stirring occasionally. As soon as the water and milk reaches boiling, reduce the heat to low and continue cooking for about 30 seconds. Prepare your noodles according to the packet instructions and drain.

Place your noodles in 2 serving bowls and pour over the curry soup. Mix lightly. Top with the bean sprouts, wakame, roasted pork and butter.

Adding butter to ramen will soften any overly strong flavours and, like cheese, it will enrich the dish for when you need something supremely comforting and a bit more indulgent.

CORN, BROCCOLI & BACON RAMEN

Serves 2

Sweetcorn (*tomorokoshi*) was actually introduced to Japan by
the Portuguese in 1579. Grown most famously in Hokkaido, by
the 1960s it had become a popular ingredient, adding a juicy
pop of sweetness to counter salty soy and miso flavours,

1 small head broccoli
4 rashers (slices) streaky bacon
1 tablespoon butter
4 tablespoons tinned sweetcorn
Pinch of sea salt
75 ml (2½ fl oz/6 tablespoons) hot water
2 x instant ramen soup sachets
   (miso flavour)
2 x 140 g (5 oz) instant ramen noodles
   (miso flavour)

Cut the broccoli into small florets and slice the bacon into strips
measuring about 5 mm (¼ in) wide.

Heat the butter in a frying pan over a low heat. When melted, add the
bacon and broccoli florets. Turn the heat up to medium and stir-fry until
the bacon is lightly crisped and the broccoli is tender. Add the sweetcorn
to the pan with a pinch of salt. Mix everything well and scatter over the
hot water and the instant ramen miso soup sachet contents. Stir-fry for
about 30 seconds, and then turn off the heat.

Make the noodles according to the instructions on the packet. Drain
and divide between 2 serving bowls. Divide the stir-fried ingredients
over each noodle bowl.

QUICK BREAKFAST RAMEN

Serves 2

A traditional Japanese breakfast can encompass up to eight separate dishes, including rice, miso, vegetables, egg, fish and pickles, but this recipe makes a delicious and speedy alternative.

1 teaspoon vegetable oil
4 rashers (slices) smoked bacon
2 medium (US large) eggs
100 g (3½ oz/1 cup) shredded Chinese cabbage
45 g (1½ oz/¼ cup) tinned sweetcorn
Sea salt and ground pepper
1 litre (35 fl oz/4¼ cups) water
2 x 140 g (5 oz) instant ramen noodles (salty/shio flavour)
2 x instant ramen soup sachets (salty/shio flavour)

Heat the vegetable oil in a frying pan. Add the bacon. When they are browned on one side, turn them over and break an egg over a pair of browned rashers. Continue to cook over a medium-low heat until the white of the egg on top of the bacon is opaque. Remove the bacon and egg from the pan to a warmed plate.

Wipe the pan with kitchen paper towels to remove some of the bacon fat (there should still be some oil residue). Heat the pan over a medium heat. Once hot, add the shredded cabbage and sweetcorn and fry for 3–4 minutes until tender. Season with salt and pepper.

Cook the instant noodles, including the soup sachet, according to the instructions on the packet. Divide the noodles and their broth between 2 serving bowls. Spoon over the fried cabbage and corn, then top with the bacon and eggs and extra black pepper, if desired.

Ramen isn't a typical breakfast meal in Japan, but Kitakata city in Fukushima Prefecture is famed for ramen and residents will eat it at any time of the day.

BUTTERY MISO RAMEN

Serves 2

If it's something quick and soothing that you are craving, this
creamy, nurturing bowl of noodles hits the spot. Simple, tasty and
satisfying for moments when you need the hug of comfort food.
Dairy products are a fairly new ingredient in Japanese cooking,
but since the 1960s, it has become more common to find cheese,
yoghurt, milk and cream both in supermarkets and in recipes.

400 ml (14 fl oz/1⅔ cups) water
2 x 140 g (5 oz) instant ramen noodles
    (miso flavour)
100 ml (3½ fl oz/scant ½ cup) fresh single
    (light) cream
1 x 150 g (5 ¼ oz) tin sweetcorn
2 x instant ramen soup sachets
    (miso flavour)
2 x instant ramen soup sachets
    (miso flavour)
2 x instant ramen oil seasoning sachets
    (if included)

TOPPINGS
Chilli Oil or Aromatic Oil (see page 30)
1–2 spring onions (scallions), sliced
Shichimi togarashi

Put the water in a saucepan, bring it the boil and add in the noodles.
When the noodles are loosened, pour in the fresh cream. Add more
cream to make it creamier, or less to make the broth thinner.

Bring back to the boil and tip in the drained sweetcorn. Turn off the heat
and stir through the instant ramen miso soup sachets.

Divide the noodles and soup between 2 serving bowls, and scatter over
the additional spice sachet from the noodles, if included. If not, drizzle
with chilli or aromatic oil. Scatter over the spring onions and *shichimi*.

It wasn't until the 1960s that the use of butter, fuelled by
Western influences, became more common in Japan.
More recently, a trend for 'butter ping cuisine' saw the
rise of melted butter poured over everyday dishes.

EASY SHIN RAMEN

Serves 2

Shin ramen or *shin ramuyen* is the Korean translation for instant spicy noodles. Super convenient, these little packets, with sachets included, can be enhanced with a few simple additions. If you are in a rush and need to take the stress out of meal preparation, then this dish is a dream. Tasty and balanced, it can be on the table in less than 10 minutes.

200 g (7 oz/3 cups prepared) Chinese cabbage
2–3 spring onions (scallions)
60 g (2 oz) peeled prawns (shrimp)
2 x 140 g (5 oz) instant ramen noodles (spicy flavour)
2 x instant ramen soup sachets (spicy flavour)

TOPPINGS
2 raw egg yolks
Shredded nori

Chop the Chinese cabbage and spring onions into bite-sized pieces. Place the cabbage and peeled prawns (shrimp) into a heat-resistant container, cover and heat in the microwave for 2–3 minutes.

In the meantime, make up the instant noodles in boiling water according to the instructions on the packet, and add the accompanying instant ramen soup sachets.

Put the cooked Chinese cabbage and prawns in a frying pan and add in the spring onions. Toss and stir-fry over a high heat to evaporate any remaining juices.

Divide the noodle soup into 2 serving bowls, and add the cabbage and prawns. Top each with a raw egg yolk and shredded nori.

TOFU, KIMCHI & CHEESE RAMEN

Serves 2

If you love the distinctive acid sharp flavour of kimchi, then this super simple recipe is for you. The addition of cheese brings a salty flavour, and although cheese is not a traditional ingredient in Japan, the rise in popularity of pizza has seen it used increasingly in numerous dishes.

2 medium (US large) eggs
300 g (10½ oz) firm tofu
160 g (6 oz/¾ cup) kimchi
60 g (2 oz/½ cup) grated Cheddar cheese
2 x 140 g (5 oz) instant ramen noodles (salty/shio flavour)
2 x instant ramen soup sachets (salty/shio flavour)

Beat the eggs in a small bowl. Dice the tofu into cubes and place them in a microwaveable bowl along with the kimchi and beaten eggs. Scatter the cheese on top and cover with cling film (plastic wrap). Microwave at 800W for 2 minutes 30 seconds.

Prepare the noodles with the soup sachets according to the instructions on the packet and divide between 2 serving bowls. Scoop the bubbling cheese, egg and tofu mixture on top.

The saltiness and richness makes cheese a great addition to more basic ramen bowls. Melt it over noodles or mix it through the noodles and broth to boost tastiness and make an instantly filling dish.

SPICY TUNA RAMEN

Serves 2

Made with everyday ingredients, this is a speedy noodle
bowl when you want maximum taste with minimum effort.
The tuna adds a helping of protein and important fish oils.
No frills, no fuss, just a tasty, nourishing meal.

1 x 70 g (2½ oz) tin tuna in oil
250 ml (8½ fl oz/1 cup) water
2 x 140 g (5 oz) instant ramen noodles
 (soy flavour)
2 x instant ramen soup sachets
 (soy flavour)

TOPPINGS
1 medium (US large) soft-boiled egg
½ cucumber, sliced into thin rounds
6 cherry tomatoes, halved lengthways

Drain the tuna, breaking it up lightly with a fork. Add the instant ramen
soup sachets to a mixing bowl and mix with the water to make a thick
saucy paste. Stir this through the tuna flakes.

Cook the instant noodles in boiling water according to the instructions
on the packet. Drain and quickly plunge into cold water.

Divide the noodles between 2 serving bowls. Top with the tuna sauce.
Finish each bowl with half an egg, the cucumber and cherry tomatoes.

Fresh tuna is highly prized and expensive in Japan, so
the tinned variety makes an affordable alternative. A
staple in sushi rolls, spiced versions adorn rice too, and
feature in speedy, no-fuss ramen dishes like this one.

CREAMY CHICKEN RAMEN

Serves 2

A one-pot wonder for when time is short but you still want something tasty and interesting to eat. Enriched with beaten egg to add creaminess and protein to the chicken flavoured noodles, make sure when adding eggs to any boiling broth you beat them first.

1 litre (35 fl oz/4¼ cups) full-fat (whole) milk
4 leaves Chinese cabbage or spring cabbage, shredded
2 x 140 g (5 oz) instant ramen noodles (chicken flavour)
2 x instant ramen soup sachets (chicken flavour)
2 medium (US large) eggs
Freshly ground black pepper

Pour the milk into a saucepan and add the shredded cabbage. Bring to a light boil and cook for 1 minute so the cabbage still has some bite.

Keep the milk and cabbage at a simmer and add in the ramen noodles and the flavour sachets. Stir well.

In a bowl, beat the eggs and then slowly tip them into the milky mixture. Stir lightly and simmer for another 2 minutes until the egg is just cooked.

Divide the cabbage, egg and noodle mixture into 2 serving bowls and season with cracked black pepper.

Shredded cabbage is widely used in Japanese cuisine, as it cuts through the richness of pork-based dishes. Napa, or Chinese cabbage, is used here but you can swap for locally available green cabbage.

ROSÉ KOREAN RAMEN

Serves 2

This intensely savoury noodle bowl became a viral hit on
Korean Twitter. Savoury Asian sausages are very similar
to Western pork varieties, but frankfurter sausages, cut
diagonally, are more commonly used in this dish.

1 white onion
6 frankfurters
1 tablespoon olive oil
1 litre (35 fl oz/4¼ cups) full-fat
    (whole) milk
1 teaspoon *gochujang* (Korean red
    chilli paste)
2 x 140 g (5 oz) instant ramen noodles
    (spicy flavour)
2 x instant ramen soup sachets
    (spicy flavour)
2 slices Cheddar cheese

Thinly slice the onion and cut the frankfurters diagonally into bite-
sized pieces. Heat the olive oil in a frying pan and fry the onions and
frankfurters for 4–5 minutes until the onion is softened.

Add the milk and *gochujang* and bring to the boil, making sure the
gochujang is well mixed in.

When the milk boils, turn it down to a simmer and add the spicy ramen
noodles straight to the pan with the contents of the soup mix sachets.
Boil for 4–5 minutes or as indicated on the packet.

Once ready, pour into a serving bowl and place the cheese slices over the
top, allowing them to melt gently.

Savoury Asian sausages are made from pork or, less
often, chicken and include livers. They are available
fresh or smoked. Cantonese types tend to be sweeter,
while Sichuan versions are spicier as they contain chilli.

PONYO'S RAMEN

Serves 2

If you are a Studio Ghibli fan, then you might want to try out the simple supper dish Ponyo and her friend Sosuke enjoy. It's a Japanese twist on ham and eggs sitting on a top of a tasty chicken broth, topped with sesame oil to give a gently sweet and nutty twist.

2 x 140 g (5 oz) instant ramen noodles
(chicken flavour)
2 x instant ramen soup sachets
(chicken flavour)
1 litre (35 fl oz/4¼ cups) water

TOPPINGS
4 slices thick-cut cooked ham
2 boiled eggs, halved
4 spring onions (scallions), sliced
1 teaspoon sesame oil (optional)

Place the chicken ramen noodles and sachet mix in 2 serving bowls and pour the hot water over the noodles.

Cover the noodles with plates or pan lids and let them sit for 3 minutes. Once done, stir gently. Top each with 2 ham slices and half an egg.

Scatter spring onions on top. Drizzle with sesame oil.

Ponyo's ramen is a simple and comforting bowl that takes you back to childhood. Of all noodle dishes in Studio Ghibli films, this is the most requested. It's an ideal recipe for newcomers to ramen cooking as all the ingredients are familiar and easy to find.

INGREDIENTS & SUPPLIERS

Here are key ingredients and specialist suppliers to aid your ramen-making. Be aware that ingredients from Asian supermarkets may not always have an English label or may be known under a different name, depending on origin.

Bonito flakes See *Katsuobushi*

Chillies Buy Asian dried red chillies, whole or in flakes, to use in seasonings, oils and cooked dishes.

Chinese glass noodles Also known as cellophane and bean thread noodles, these are made from mung bean and become translucent when cooked.

Daikon The general name given to radish in Japan, it is also known by the Chinese name of mooli. This large, white Asian radish is milder, sweeter and less piquant than its smaller Western varieties.

Doenjang A spicy Korean soybean paste made from fermented soybeans and brine. It is usually stir-fried in oil to release its intense flavour.

Furikake A blend of dried nori, toasted sesame seeds, sugar and salt, this seasoning is a popular seasoning for rice bowls and noodle dishes.

Gochugaru A Korean red chilli powder with smoky, slightly sweet, fruity notes and a hot kick.

Gochujang A spicy but sweet Korean red chilli fermented paste; add a touch in the base of your bowl or stir into your broth for a kick of heat.

Kaiware These daikon seed sprouts are used in Asian salads and sushi, but cress or mustard sprouts or microgreens can be substituted.

Kamaboko Made from puréed white fish formed into a roll or cake, it can be sliced and used to top a bowl of ramen. It has a distinctive pink outer edge. The version known as *narutomaki* has a pink swirl.

Karashi takana Pickled mustard greens add texture and mild sour and spicy taste.

Katsuobushi Commonly known as bonito, it is available as flakes or a stock powder. It is a fermented and dried skipjack tuna with a distinct umami taste.

Kimchi A fiery fermented cabbage dish from Korea that combines sour with tanginess. It is traditionally eaten as a side dish but is a popular ramen topping.

Kombu A type of sea kelp available in largish flat strips, it is often used in broths or stocks, adding an ocean-like, savoury and salty note to a dish.

Mayu A rich, sweet-tasting burnt (black) garlic oil that adds complexity of flavour to ramen.

Menma Fermented or pickled bamboo shoots that have first been dried in the sun, menma are sold in jars or vacuum-packed.

Mentsuyu An intensely flavoured, liquid Chinese soup stock concentrate, made from bonito flakes, kombu and soy sauce, it is used in much the same way as a stock (bouillon) cube.

Mirin A sweet rice wine used as a seasoning, glazing agent and to balance salty flavours.

Miso Produced by fermenting soybeans into a thick paste, miso adds a deeply umami flavour to sauces and is mixed with dashi stock for soup or ramen. It is available in paste or powder form.

Mushrooms Dried mushrooms, such as shiitake and wood ear (*kikurage*), impart delicious flavour and texture to ramen. To rehydrate, soak in enough water to cover for at least 20 minutes. When soft, squeeze out the water and remove the stalks (stems).

Nam pla A Thai fish sauce made from salted and fermented fish.

Nori A flat dried seaweed leaf that can be cut into a square to top ramen. Shredded nori is sold in packs.

Ramen Chukamen, or ramen, noodles are available in long, curled and flattened versions. For the recipes in this book, 140 g (5 oz) single-portion instant noodle packets are used; if you are using a different weight, please adjust the recipe accordingly or break the noodles into 140 g portions.

Saké Use cooking saké, which is lower in alcohol and more intensely concentrated than the alcoholic drink. It is also much less expensive.

Sesame The oil is used to cook and flavour food while the seeds can be used ground for thickening soups or whole (and toasted) for a seasoning.

Shichimi togarashi A traditional Japanese spice mix to scatter over food, *shichimi* usually contains seven spices, with red chilli being the most dominant.

Shiso Also known as *oba* or perilla leaves, they are often used in raw fish dishes in Japan. They have an elegant, unique flavour akin to aniseed.

Soba A popular, thin Japanese noodle, soba is made from buckwheat and looks a little more 'rustic' in colouring than other noodle types. They work equally well in hot soups or chilled with dipping sauces.

Somen These are super-thin noodles made from wheat flour dough mixed with vegetable oil.

Tobanjan A Sichuan-style paste made from broad beans and a special blend of chillies. It can be used as a dipping sauce or to add a little heat to broths and stir-fried meats and vegetables.

Tobiko Often used to top sushi, this colourful flying fish roe imparts a salty, smoky taste.

Udon Made from wheat flour, these are much thicker than other ramen noodles.

Umeboshi A pickled Japanese ume fruit that is extremely sour and salty but works well with pork.

Wakame Thinner strips of seaweed often used in miso-based soups and dishes, adding an ocean-like, savoury and salty note to a dish.

Yuzu A yellow citrus fruit that is a popular souring agent in Japan, adding a tang of citrus to dishes. Both the zest and juices can be used and it is more fragrant than its lemon and lime counterparts.

Yuzu kosho A fermented spice paste made with salted chilli peppers and the rind of the yuzu fruit. It is used to add zesty flavour to light broths, added to ramen as a condiment or stirred into the broth.

UK SUPPLIERS

Chef's Wonderland

chefswonderland.com

A website dedicated to Japanese cuisine around the world, it not only supplies a list of Japanese cooking suppliers but also Japanese grocery stores in the UK.

Clearspring

www.clearspring.co.uk

Supplies authentic Japanese specialties and organic fine foods, including pastes, noodles, sea vegetables, miso, condiments and plant-based alternatives.

H Mart

hmart.co.uk/hmart.com

Source for Asian groceries, fresh and chilled food, and equipment, including a big range of branded dried noodles and ramen, sauces, spices and snacks.

HiYou

hiyou.co

Offers fresh and seasonal Japanese grocery items, as well as frozen items such as noodles, wonton wrappers and seafood, and food cupboard items.

Japan Centre

japancentre.com

From noodles to miso, condiments and seasonings, there is a range of grocery items available from their website, including dashi stock powder, a variety of noodles, *shichimi togarashi* and frozen fishcakes.

Natural Natural

natural-natural.shop

With shops in London, which sell fresh meat, fish and sashimi, this is a wonderful source for frozen meat, fish and noodles, as well as ramen, tofu, condiments, seasonings, dashi stocks, saké and gifts.

Oriental Mart

orientalmart.co.uk

Supplier of Asian products with a Japanese category, including one for *furikake*, miso paste and seasoning sachets such as dried bonito flakes.

Starry Mart

starrymart.co.uk

Supplier of Asian products with a Japanese category. As well as selling a variety of noodles, it sells instant noodle products, dried shrimp, pickled products such as umeboshi and pickled ginger, and frozen seafood.

Sushi Sushi

sushisushi.co.uk

Supplier of premium Japanese ingredients, categories include seaweed, yuzu, miso, noodles and seaweed.

Vegetarian Express

www.vegex.co.uk

Online supplier of authentic vegetarian Japanese products, including shichimi togarashi.

US SUPPLIERS

Just Asian Food

justasianfood.com

Includes a category for Japanese foods such as noodles, seasonings, sauces and soup bases.

Just Hungry

justhungry.com

Website dedicated to Japanese recipes that has links to Japanese grocery stores in the United States and its territories.

Kokoro Care

kokorocares.com/collections/market-michi-no-eki

Supplies natural products made in Japan without chemicals, from dashi packets to seasonings and noodles, as well as care packages fill with artisan Japanese food; they will delivery worldwide but have a minimum order to do so.

Umami Insider

umami-insider.store

Specialty store supplying high-quality ingredients from Japan, including storecupboard staples such as seaweed, seasonings such as shichimi togarashi, and vegetables such as umeboshi and dried shiitake.

Yamibuy

yamibuy.com

Extensive grocery range of Japanese, Korean and Chinese products and ingredients.

INDEX

ajitama 37
ajitsuke tamago 18, 37
almond milk 56
Ando, Momofoku 9
apple cider vinegar 29
Aromatic Oil 30, 77, 156
arugula *see* rocket
aubergine 94, 135
Aubergine Miso Ramen 135

bacon 91, 152, 154
bamboo shoots 21, 76, 96, 128
    see also menma
bean sprouts 21, 39, 49, 70, 72, 78,
    106, 134, 151
bean thread noodles *see* Chinese
    glass noodles
beef bones 11
beef ramen 65, 98–103
Beef Ramen, Warm 98
bok choy *see* pak choi
bonito flakes 11, 16, 28, 120, 124
bonito stock powder 117
bowls 11
Breakfast Ramen, Quick 154
broccoli 128, 152
broths and soups 9, 11, 26–8, 139
buckwheat noodles 13
building ramen bowls 9, 10–11
butter 151
Buttery Miso Ramen 156

cabbage 21
Carbonara Ramen 91
carrot 50, 128, 132
celery 77, 132
cellophane noodles *see* Chinese
    glass noodles
Chanpon 82
Char Siu Pork Ramen 150
chashu 18, 32, 33, 39, 44, 66, 116
cheese 91, 142, 148, 158, 162
chicken bones 11, 16, 26
Chicken Chashu 33
Chicken Curry Ramen 50
Chicken Dashi 26
chicken glass noodle soup base 82
chicken ramen 41, 42–56, 58
Chicken Wing Ramen 54
Chige Ramen 116
Chilled Ramen 96
chilli bean paste 49, 77, 78, 89
chilli flakes 22, 116
Chilli Miso Ramen 42
Chilli Oil 30, 48, 56, 88, 89, 128,
    131, 156
chillies, red 57, 78, 116, 124
Chinese cabbage 22, 132, 154,
    157, 161
Chinese chives 72, 78, 80, 96,
    116, 135
Chinese five-spice powder 150
Chinese glass noodles 14, 78, 100

Chinese longevity noodles 6
Chinese watermelon radish 22
chukamen ramen noodles 13
clams, baby 116
classic dishes 16–17
Coconut Curry Ramen 84
coconut milk 84
cold ramen 45, 48, 96, 131, 143
Cold Shio Ramen 143
Cold Tan Tan Noodles, Cold 131
Collagen Ramen 44
condiments 30–1
conpoy 29, 109
coriander, ground 60, 110
coriander (cilantro) leaves 84, 106,
    110, 114, 144
Corn, Broccoli & Bacon
    Ramen 152
Cosy Winter Dry Ramen 94
Crab & Egg Ramen 108
Crab Ramen 106
cream, single 156
Creamy Chicken Ramen 48;
    (instant) 161
cress 112, 122
cucumber 76, 90, 130, 160
curry pastes 50, 110
curry powders 84, 151

daikon 22, 45, 78
dan dan 56, 131

dango 84
dashi 9, 11, 26–8, 38, 139
Diet Ramen 134
doenjang 76
doubanjiang 102, 131
dressings, sesame 45
dried noodles 15
dry ramen 94
Duck Dipping Ramen 62
duck ramen 41, 57, 59–63

eggplant *see* aubergine
eggs 91, 108, 134, 139, 157, 158, 161
    boiled 18, 86, 109, 130, 143, 160, 164
    fried 154
    marinated 18, 37, 56, 66, 96, 106
enoki mushrooms 21, 144
extra helpings 13

Filipino pancit noodles 9
fish ramen 114, 117, 120,
    122
fishcake 21, 82, 117
Fish Dashi 28
fish roe 117
five-spice powder 150
Floating Egg Ramen 139
Fluffy Egg Ramen 72
frankfurters 162
fresh noodles 14
furikake 23, 84, 136, 144

garlic 26, 30, 88, 128, 139
garlic oil, black 72
garlic-soy sauce 135
Get Well Soon Ramen 132
Ginger Fish Ramen 120
ginger root 22, 26, 33, 76, 77, 78, 89,
    94, 102, 120, 122, 124, 132, 136
gluten-free noodles 13
gochugaru 23, 30
gochujang 23, 49, 57, 86, 90,
    116, 162
goma dare 89
green tea soba 15

ham 164
himokawa noodles
hiyashi-chuka 96
honey 66
hyamugi noodles 14

ice, crushed 143
Indonesian noodles 9
ingredients, specialist 23
instant noodles 7, 9, 15
instant ramen 147–65

Jaja Ramen 90
Japan, ramen in 6–7, 9, 10
Japanese curry paste 50
Japanese curry powder 151
Japanese egg-drop soup 139

Japanese Kewpie mayo noodles 9
Japanese sesame paste 130
Japanese sesame sauce 89

kaedama 13
kaiware radish sprouts 112, 122
kake udon noodles 14
kakitamajiru 139
kale, curly 124
kamaboko 21, 82, 117
kanikama 108
kansui 13
karashi takana 98
katsuobushi 11, 16, 28, 120, 124
kikurage 21, 98
kimchi 9, 22, 68, 158
Kimchi Ramen 68
King Prawn Miso Ramen 112
kishimen noodles 14
kombu 11, 21, 28, 29, 120, 136
Korean BBQ sauce 68
Korean hot-dog ramen 9
Korean thin noodles 9, 131, 143

la-yu see Chilli Oil
lettuce leaves 45
lime wedges 100

mandarin orange zest 102
mayu 72
Meat-Free Carbonara 142

menma 21, 39, 70
mentsuyu 23, 48, 68, 73, 88, 94
microgreens 112, 122
mien noodles 14
milk, full-fat (whole) 124, 130, 151, 161, 162
mirin 29, 33, 37, 135
Miso Milk Curry Ramen 151
Miso Mince 36
miso paste 36, 70, 89, 106, 112, 136, 138
miso powder 42, 48, 131
Miso Ramen 16, 77
miso sauce 10
mooli see daikon
Mozzarella & Tomato Ramen 148
mung bean flour 14
Mushroom Miso Ramen 138
Mushroom Tempura Ramen 144
mushrooms
    dried 21
    enoki 21, 144
    oyster 138
    shiitake 11, 21, 28, 29, 36, 76, 86, 90, 128, 138, 144
    shimeji 36, 134, 138, 144
    wood ear 21, 98
mustard leaves, pickled 98

nam pla 22, 57, 84, 110
Naruto Ramen 70
narutomaki 21, 70, 82, 106, 112
nasu dengaku 135
neri goma 89, 130
niboshi 11, 16, 28
noodle production in Japan 7, 9
noodles 9, 13–15
nori 21, 70, 151

oils 30–1
One-Pot Ramen, Addictive 73
onion 21, 28, 128
origins of ramen 6, 10
oyster mushrooms 138
oyster sauce 32, 39, 54

pak choi 54, 98, 102, 122
parsley, flat-leaf 148
pastes
    chilli bean 49, 77, 78, 89
    curry 50, 110
    miso 36, 70, 89, 106, 112, 136, 138
    sesame 130
    soybean 76, 102
peanut butter 130
pepper, black 30, 161
Pho-Style Beef Ramen 100
pink ume soba 15
Ponyo's Ramen 164
pork bones 11, 16
Pork Chashu 18, 32, 39, 44, 116
Pork Chashu Ramen 66
Pork Dashi 26
pork mince 36
Pork Mince Broth, Hearty 76
pork ramen 65, 66–97, 150
potato starch 76
Prawn Ramen 110
prawns (shrimp) 110, 112, 157
Pumpkin Miso Ramen 136

radish 22
Ramen Recipe, Basic 38
Ramen Salad 45
restaurants 7–9, 39
rice bran oil 30

rice flour 14
rocket 45
Rosé Korean Ramen 162

Salmon & Pak Choi Ramen 122
salt seasoning see Shio Tare
Salty Scallop Ramen 109
sardines, dried 11, 16, 28
sauces
    fish 22, 57, 84
    garlic-soy 135
    Japanese sesame 89
    Korean BBQ 68
    miso 10
    oyster 32, 39, 54
    sesame 89
    tahini 56
    teriyaki 57
    see also soy sauce
sausages, savoury Asian 162
scallops, dried 29, 109
sea bass 120
sea bream 120
seafood & fish ramen 105–25
Seafood Ramen 117
sea kelp 11, 21, 28, 29, 120, 136
sesame dressing 45
sesame oil 30
sesame paste 130
sesame sauce 89
sesame seeds 23, 49, 68, 86, 88, 94, 114, 116, 122, 143
shallots 57
Shantung soup seasoning 77
shichimi togarashi 23, 62, 70, 94, 110, 144, 148, 156
shiitake mushrooms 11, 21, 28, 29, 36, 76, 86, 90, 128, 138, 144

shimeji mushrooms 36, 134, 138, 144

Shin Ramen, Easy 157

shin ramuyen 157

shina soba 6

shio ramen 16, 143

Shio Ramen, Cold 143

Shio Tare 29

shiro see white miso

shiso flavourings 23, 52

shojin ryori 130

Shoyu Ramen 16, 39

shrimp, dried 29

Silken Tofu Ramen 130

soba noodles 13, 15

somen noodles 13, 143

soups *see* broths and soups

Soy-marinated Egg 37, 56, 66, 96, 106

soy sauce 10
    dark 16, 23, 29, 32, 36, 37
    Japanese 33, 39, 66, 89, 102, 108, 112, 135
    light 16, 23, 29
    sweet 36

soya milk 48, 56, 70, 122, 131, 151

soybean paste 76, 102

Spice-seasoned Egg 37, 70, 117

Spicy Korean Ramen 86

Spicy Tuna Ramen 160

spinach 21, 52, 56, 86, 91, 114, 132

spring onion (scallion) 21, 26, 30, 37, 44, 62, 66, 80, 88, 100, 102, 109, 116, 128, 136, 139, 156, 157, 164

Squid & Kale Ramen 124

sriracha 22, 57

sùmiàn noodles *see* somen noodles

Super Spicy Noodles 88

Sweet & Spicy Duck Ramen 57

sweetcorn 21, 50, 82, 152, 154

tahini 56, 89, 130

Tahini Ramen 89

tahini sauce 56

Taiwan Beef Noodles 102

Taiwan Ramen 78

Tan Tan Men 56

Tan Tan Noodles, Cold 131

tare 9, 10

Tare Sauce 29

tataki 114

tempura flour 144

teriyake sauce 57

Thai basil 100

Thai chilli powder 110

Thai red curry paste 110

tobanjan 49, 77, 78, 89

tobiko 117

Tofu & Chicken Ramen 49

Tofu, Kimchi & Cheese Ramen 158

tofu 49, 116, 130, 158

togarashi 23, 62, 70, 88, 94, 110, 144, 148, 156

Tomato & Chicken Ramen 52

tomato juice 52

tomato ketchup 52

tomatoes 84, 88, 96, 148, 160

tomorokoshi 21, 50, 82, 152, 154

tonkotsu ramen 16, 26

toppings 9, 11, 18–23, 32–7

transparency, broth 38

transparent noodles *see* Chinese glass noodles

tsukemen ramen 16, 62

tsuyu see mentsuyu

Tuna Tataki Ramen 114

tuna, tinned 160

udon noodles 14, 98, 102, 106, 117

umami flavour 10, 11, 16, 21

umeboshi 22

Vegan Dashi 28

Vegan Mince 36

vegan & vegetarian ramen 21, 127–45

Vegetable Garden Ramen 128

Vietnamese noodles 9, 14

wakame 21, 42, 150, 151

wanton wrappers (skins) 80

Warm Beef Ramen 98

wasabi flavourings 23

white miso 16
    paste 36, 70, 89, 106, 112, 136, 138
    powder 42, 48, 131

Wonton Ramen 80

wood ear mushrooms 21, 98

yakatori 60

Yuzu Duck Ramen 60

yuzu kosho 23, 60

yuzu purée 73

yuzu shichimi 94

ABOUT THE AUTHOR

I became a chef because I enjoy cooking, eating and watching people gathering and laughing around food. I believe food brings people together, which brings happiness.

Many people don't cook these days because of their busy schedules. However, cooking is very therapeutic and creative and doesn't need to take too much time.

Through this book, I hope more people will appreciate making as well as consuming food.

Happy cooking!

Makiko Sano

Makiko Sano is a Japanese chef, author and teacher who specializes in creating delicious and healthy Japanese cuisine. She is also a personal chef and party creator, so she knows how to make your event special. Her cookbooks are full of recipes that are easy to follow and will help you create amazing meals for your family and friends.

She runs Suzu House in London, which offers an intimate dining experience combined with skilfully prepared, traditional Japanese cuisine, and also hands-on cooking classes that will teach you how to make delicious sushi, ramen and more at home.

Makiko Sano is the perfect source of culinary inspiration for anyone who wants to learn more about Japanese cooking. Thanks to her, you can now enjoy the best of Japan in your own home.

See more at www.makikosano.co.uk and https://thesuzuhouse.com

CREDITS

ACKNOWLEDGEMENTS

The publisher would like the following:
Emma Bannister for her concise editorial,
problem-solving and fact-checking.

Simon Smith Photography at
simonsmithphotography.co.uk
for props, backgrounds and food photography.

Pippa Leon for home economy and food styling;
Morag Farquhar for props styling. James Pople
for an inspired cover and interior design.

PICTURE CREDITS